WHERE IS SAINT GEORGE?

WHERE IS SAINT GEORGE?

PAGAN IMAGERY IN ENGLISH FOLKSONG

Bob Stewart

BLANDFORD PRESS
LONDON · NEW YORK · SYDNEY

This edition published in the UK 1988 by
Blandford Press, Artillery House, Artillery Row, London SW1P 1RT

Copyright © 1977 and 1988 R. J. Stewart

Distributed in the United States by
Sterling Publishing Co, Inc.
2 Park Avenue, New York, NY 10016

British Library Cataloguing in Publication Data

Stewart, Bob
  Where is Saint George? : pagan imagery in
  English folksong. 2nd ed.
  1. Folk songs in English. Pagan symbolism -
  Sources of data : South-west English folk
  songs
  I. Title
  784.4'9423

ISBN 0 7137 2030 1

Printed in Guildford by Biddles.

CONTENTS

Preface

The history of this book is as follows: in 1976 I appeared on a television programme in England, and talked briefly about the symbols and imagery found in folksong, and how this related to the broader field of myth legend and tradition. At that time, I was a touring musician and occasional composer, with no thoughts of writing a book. The day after my television appearance I received a call from Tony Adams of Moonraker Press; he suggested in his modest but persistent manner that I could (and therefore should) write a book for him to publish, elaborating upon those ideas that I had touched upon during the interview.

I was in the middle of location musical directing for a Tony Richardson film (*Joseph Andrews*) but somehow found time to prepare a manuscript. Within a year, I had worked the material into shape, and it was duly published in Britain and in the USA. The book proved popular, and even found its way into the supplementary reading lists for educational courses ranging from literature to psychology.

In the intervening twelve years I have written a further sixteen books, and no longer tour as a performer, though I still compose and record. Many of those books have dealt in depth with subjects that are hinted at in *Where is Saint George*? But I would not wish to rewrite any of this book, only to state that the discography and the reading list are now replaced and supplemented by lists in my other books.

There is a tremendous interest in tradition, esoteric symbolism, legend and myth, far greater now than when this book was first published. I am therefore very pleased that this new paperback edition has appeared to meet the demand, for it is still cited in new publications and has not been available for several years.

Regrettably Tony Adams died before any of my other books were published, so he did not see the material that he helped to unleash upon the world: this new edition is dedicated to him.

R. J. Stewart
Bath 1988

Introduction

The basic theory put forward in this book is simple. Folk songs and music retain the roots of primitive magic and religion. This is not a new or startling suggestion but the method of approach suggested in the following pages reveals a continuity in the folk material, and a degree of magical inheritance that is very wide and not restricted to curious examples or isolated songs without context.

The songs examined were all collected in the West of England, with reference to their relatives in other parts of the world. The conclusions are not limited to any area, however, although fine details will vary from region to region when considering historical facts, racial distribution, and localised folklore still surviving.

The theory suggests that certain basic *images* found in traditional poetry, and certain musical phrases linked inseparably with the songs, are those common to Celtic and pre-Celtic worship, later absorbed by Christian development. These images have continued to survive in the imagination of the native tradition virtually until the present day, but are now undergoing a major period of stress and possible change. The suggestion is supported by various forms of evidence, drawing upon known examples of British mythology, classical parallels, psychology, early church records, oral lore, and poetical intuition. The general discussion is not complex and may be followed without constant recourse to learned works, so detailed footnotes are not given. The bibliography of this subject is immense; examples have been given for each section whenever relevant, followed by a general list.

No amount of study, however, is a substitute for listening to folk-song and music, or at second best reading the ballads and songs collected from folk singers. The songs should never be separated from their music, or their true effect and meaning is shattered. With this important point in mind a short discography has been suggested, mainly with a view to avoiding certain commercial products which damage representation of folksongs, and confuse appreciation. This does not imply 'purism' but it is essential to be very selective until a general realisation of the true nature of our native music is established in the mind. True British folksongs are known by their *feel* as any folksong collector will tell you, and this intuitive level is only reached by a great deal of listening to the songs themselves. Eventually the spirit of the tradition will regenerate in the listener's mind, until it is possible to pinpoint fake or extraneous material very easily, without recourse to reference works other than for detailed confirmation.

The same rule applies to folk tales, myths and ancient lore in general; once again, there is no substitute for the real thing. This means of identifying true folk material may sound like the old alchemists' trick 'to make gold you first have to have gold', but there is no reason to despair. The gold is already present in our own consciousness, as a deep and ever-present part of our racial inheritance. Today it has been overlaid by uncertain educational methods, by media-conditioning, and by the stresses of our rather odd society; but it is still present, and responds positively when summoned. Our ancestors would have said that the gods may be called by the right invocations, but whether we use magical or psychological terminology, we all have this imaginative and partly racial stream of awareness, which is usually represented by folk and fairy tales, old lore and songs, or the analogous tales known as myths. Material of this sort is very satisfying though not necessarily logical and has a great therapeutic value, especially in a society almost utterly divorced from the relationship between human and environment, soul and seasons, which racial lore represents. Much of the discussion is necessarily 'religious' but this is through necessity, and not by deliberate policy. There is no religious attitude behind the theory, and it is not an offering or upholding or even a suggestion of revival of any type of pseudo-pagan cult. Times and events form their religion spontaneously, despite periods of adroit manipulation. The basic urges of all religions are the same, and their form degenerates in the same way, returning to the imagination from which such forms emerge. By 'imagination' we should mean that area of our consciousness which generates images in response to stimuli, images that are the prototypes of forces in action, analogous modes representing energy as form. This imagination should not be confused with the notions or passing fancies that are its poor relatives.

It might be suggested that much of the argument given here is anti-Christian. This is not the case, though indeed the actions of state or church authorities of any name are damning enough within themselves, if they can be traced. As the bulk of our documented history falls within the Christian era, and is supplied through Christian sources, it is hardly surprising that all the tricks and suppressions common to any power-faction are therefore Christian in origin. Politics do not affect faith or true religious inspiration, as we shall see from the native traditions that survived right into the present century. Politics of any sort hardly affect the common people of any country, for there are more important life-issues to get on with. Today, the areas previously represented by the racial images examined in this book are being rapidly destroyed, and we do not yet know what will regenerate in their place. Neither the revived pagan nor the staunch Christian should find personal insult in the theory proposed here, as it is anthropological and does not deny anyone their personal beliefs or practices.

Evidence suggests that the majority of the British people, particularly those in the western parts of the country less open to invasion by arms and faith, were not Christians, but retained a loose and general attachment to the Celtic and even pre-Celtic divine images. As time passes, so does conscious ritual devolve into folk-lore, unless retained by deliberate effort after it has lost meaning. At this folk level the images and spirit of the native worship remain sometimes consciously, sometimes spontaneously but quite unaffected by external religious decree, and extremely difficult to eradicate.

Occasionally this deep level of imagery may take a national external form, such as the development of the cult of St George, or the period of the cult of the Blessed Virgin, or the present trend for popular singers to appear on stage as ritualistic figures. The recent reaching out after exotic and commercially inspired pseudo-Eastern religions is another manifestation of the national impulse to look for a Divine Son, faith in Christ having been shattered. If we trace this particular influence back to the last century we may find it to have a political origin, though today it is good business. If we, as people, were more aware of our true images we would waste less time and money on unsatisfactory substitutes. Names and cults are irrelevant, but the manner in which we respond to being alive ought to be important.

The theory therefore may have some human value, as well as being a study of curious and hitherto obscure lore.

This is not an exhaustive factual study. The branches upon the tree of symbols are innumerable, and no work of words can possibly cover them all. What is intended here is that the flow of the theory, and the concepts within it, draws upon a deliberately limited number of examples, the group of West-country folksongs analysed. The ramifications of related songs and lore, and the many reference-works applicable, are referred to from time to time but there is no intention of repeating existing printed works. Some of the ideas suggested may seem surprising but evidence for them is clear within the reference-works listed, and more important, is clear within folksong and lore itself.

Many pieces of supporting evidence have no doubt been missed, and numerous songs other than those quoted could have been brought in as examples. The aim is not to clear the tree of fruit, but to point out where it may be found, and how to climb from branch to branch. Once a realisation of the basic theory has been established, evidence occurs in the most surprising places, and the problem is one of exclusion rather than of hunting for relevant facts and examples.

Many of the important points discussed, such as the derivation of plain-song from pagan chant-systems, or the origin of the cult of St George, demand long and careful expositions in their own right. Sections such as these are not expanded at great length for this very reason, but are intended to hold the seeds of a large number of concepts and pieces of evidence which may be followed up at will.

No attempt has been made to re-write or analyse existing explanations of folksong or Celtic lore and myth, for it is generally assumed that the reader is familiar with some of this basic material. If he or she is not, then it is easily found and read, and even a temporary lack of grounding in folk-lore or music does not affect the understanding of the ideas proposed here.

What is vital is to be familiar with your own native mythology and poetry—nothing else will ever be a satisfactory substitute.

The Tradition

At one time, not long past, folksongs were regarded as being the by-products of dull unlettered peasants. Folk music, lore and song were supposed to be the crude entertainments of the bucolic and drink-sodden masses. This view is still held by a few classicists, but anyone with the slightest interest in music, poetry and song, and the development of expression and communication through these forms, is aware today that folksong is both the origin and the storehouse of vital root-material. The beauty of many folk melodies has become an axiom, and it is generally accepted that folksongs contain and retain ancient lore. This concept is becoming so familiar that it is hardly ever challenged; a dangerous state to be in!

Studies of folksongs and folk-lore vary greatly. They range from the close literary type of analysis developed in the nineteenth century, of which the work of Professor Francis Child is the major example, to the poetic and mythological synthesis epitomised by Robert Graves' book *White Goddess* in this century. Earlier studies and collections of folk customs and ballads tend to treat the material as being a collection of curiosities, either for exploitation by adaptation and commercialisation, or as quaint forms of peasant history and amusement. The literary and poetic extremes of viewpoint mark the boundaries of a vast territory of speculation and knowledge, ranging from intensive intellectual and literary research of a quantitative nature to qualitative interpretation that merges into mysticism.

Neither Graves nor Child, of course, dealt strictly with folksong in its own right, as one work is a study of myths and poetic symbol-systems, while the other is a superb example of obsessive cataloguing. Curious folk-lore has been collected, annotated, expounded upon, analysed, criticised, re-written and generally booted about for a very, very long time. This process develops as soon as professional literacy or musical ability and function evolve within any culture. Material often passes from the oral tradition into the professional repertoire, and is known occasionally to have passed in the opposite direction. The primary difference of method lies in the strictly oral nature of the material and its retention. Eventually the formal study of folk-lore and music becomes a demanding entity in itself, often obscuring the native material from which it has developed.

Despite tacit agreement that folksong contains ancient lore, very little direct analysis of this lore has been carried out with exclusive reference to folk *songs*. While folk-lore, ritual, dance, festivities and customs have received enormous attention, folksongs have not, despite massive works of reference and cross-reference and collections of songs in a quantitative manner. The reasons for this lack of attention are clear.

Folksong by nature is very stark and simple in content (though not in style). It is fairly easy to analyse and catalogue in a statistical or stylistic manner, but quite difficult to study its content in its own right. In contrast, folk ritual and customs, such as mummers' plays, seasonal festivals, ritual dancing, present an immediate and highly colourful source of obvious material to work with. The very subtle simplicity of folksong, and a certain general redundancy of a large body of romantic folksongs, makes a symbolic study formidable. Such a study generally moves in two main directions. The first is that of simple listing and citing of curious material found in certain songs and ballads. Works of this sort give loosely related samples, in a generally statistical manner, of superstitions, early beliefs and habits, fairy faith, and similar material. This type is the most general example of folksong text examination and commentary available. The second method of working encompasses the first, and consists of the discovery and expression of broad mythological, religious and symbolic forms within folksong plots. Any study of this sort is naturally dependent on previous work dealing with mythical and magical symbolism, usually of the statistical scholarly type. Classic studies of magic and religion, such as Frazer's *Golden Bough*, are essentially works completed in a vacuum. This does not imply any diminishing of their value, but even the monumental works of great scholars can only be exercises until they are related to human life. The aim of carrying such research through into folksong is to clarify such a living relationship.

Traditional song—that is, genuine folksong from a living oral tradition—is the natural expression of a people's own music and poetry. Such songs spring from and reflect the nature of the life of those same people, not just as an environmental relationship, but their inner life, shown through certain symbols and motifs, uniquely racial, yet with significance far beyond crude national characteristics. Such songs are not mere curiosities; they are the deep imaginative basis of all poetry and music, all art and religion, and could be said poetically to contain the seeds of our souls. If the vast resources of the study of myth and general schools of symbolism can be applied to folksong and produce results, we may have a valuable tool to put to use for the understanding, not merely of the songs themselves, but of our ancestors, and perhaps of ourselves. This is not by any means a romantic or escapist notion, for folksongs are far closer to our modern selves than we usually realise. It is often assumed that traditional songs and music, lore and ways of living are the evidence and remains of a lost or fossilised age. The current commercialised revival of interest in folk music is broadly based upon a dream of escape into 'the good old days' with the accompanying assumption that such songs are lost and represent a frozen and stylised 'past'. With this vague but generally accepted concept lives, paradoxically, the idea that 'real' tradition still 'lives' and can be found and noted from isolated persons, usually near to death from extreme old age. This belief is often used to justify the folky escapism, and occasionally as a lever for introducing faked songs and tales into the commercial revival repertoire, and more criminally into publication.

Both of these loose but widely held beliefs are quite wrong, and actively contribute to the appalling lack of true relationship with our own traditions that has developed rapidly in the last 50 years. Folksong, or any other aspect of a tradition, is not part of a lost era. Most traditional material is extremely difficult to date by normal historical methods, and it is almost impossible to give a point of origin to any one song or folk activity. The documented material or dated texts that do exist, such as early collections, notes on folk customs, printed broadsheets and derived information from other sources, merely show that the contents were in practice at the date of the documentation. It is also very difficult to show when any aspect of a tradition dies out—for there is never any conscious 'last time' for a ritual or 'last singer' of a certain song. Such material quietly fades away, and is often not missed for some long time. Folk music and lore appears and disappears in human conscious use with no historical perspective whatsoever. A body of folk material will contain units from many quite separate eras and points of view; modern entertainments live in the same house as ballads of an indefinable age, yet undeniably ancient. In some cases ancient mythological themes are found with modern melodies (see *The Two Magicians*), and distinctive archaic airs are sung for relatively recent political broadsheets, such as *The Bonny Bunch of Roses, O.*

A tradition is actually a living process with neither beginning nor ending, although it can undergo periods of severe disruption, as at the present time. The dream that decrepit country singers can still be hunted out of isolated villages and produce exciting variants or rare songs is rather naive. The majority of folksongs, in England at any rate, were collected in the present century before 1930, and even before the First World War collectors were lamenting that they could only find songs and lore from elderly people, and that younger generations were already being educated out of their tradition and rejecting it for new values and ways of life imposed by commercial necessity. This change of attitude was greatly accelerated between the wars, until the emergence of the Welfare State and enlightened technology finally disrupted the already weakened oral tradition. Today folksongs are merely another light entertainment often carried out by professionals, and ruthlessly exploited wherever possible for profit. The vision of Cecil Sharp and Ralph Vaughan Williams, both of whom worked towards a national resurgence of interest in folk-music over half-a-century ago, has gone sadly astray. This does not mean, however, that the tradition is dead, but that it is undergoing a period of considerable stress. A national tradition, the body of group life-experience expressing itself, never fully dies but alters as any organic structure will change.

Why then should we waste our time in close analysis of a group of defunct songs? The reasons for such work ought to be better than a mere revelation of obscure scholarship; but can a tradition that has been heavily attacked and damaged be of any real value to us?

The question is answered by certain clear indications within our own society. Reversion to a tradition does not mean a return to out-moded ways of life, nor does it mean the spurious 'nationalism' or 'tradition' as prostituted by politicians. The vast amount of research done on traditional material in recent years, and the thousands of records and publications, show that its value is appreciated on both intellectual and artistic levels. The contemporary revival of folksong performance shows a distinct need for material of this sort, where small independent groups of people meet together to play and listen to their own natural music, rather than to be force-fed with high-volume goods for indiscriminating consumers. Yet the real need is deeper than this, for the overall problems of our civilisation show the rapid results of immense technical advances shooting far ahead of the understanding level of almost all of the population. This new knowledge seems to be generally put to use to calm an over-populated and under-educated world. The overwhelming sense of confusion and inadequacy felt by many people today is not simply due to economic fumbling and political ineptitude, or blatant corruption, but stems from the deeper disruption of the life tradition, the separation of individuals from their racial inner reality. The situation is similar to that of plant development, where a chemical stimulus can cause a great spurt in growth, but without its balance—natural factors being harmoniously related—the plant will 'outgrow itself' and then die.

These natural factors, vital traditional material, can be found and identified in the study of folksong and folk-lore which has been collected. If a new understanding of such factors is achieved, they can be recognised in modern life, often in curious disguise, sometimes used to suppress rather than to inspire. If it is at all possible to draw conclusions from tradition about our racial characteristics, we may have the means of building a bridge between the broken life-pattern of the past and the present. This is not a false or contrived conclusion, for the small handful of songs used as examples in the following pages were all collected from people in the West of England in the present century, yet all show clearly the symbols of a racial mythology and psychology that extends unbroken from pre-Christian times. This underground stream of symbolism is the evidence for a racial 'unconscious', an analogous mode of thought that flows behind or beyond our group existence. The obvious value of material of this sort need hardly be stressed.

It will be found that the tradition takes forms that are at first surprising, and not necessarily those expected by modern reasoning or intellect.

The geographically English and West-country location of songs used as examples does not limit the field to localised conclusions. The mainstream of ballads involved are not only national, but international, in currency. The general pattern of survival of pagan material is found all over the world in any aspect of any folk culture—and the information derived from a handful of Western English songs holds good for the entire English-speaking and European peoples. Lore of this sort may simply be divided into two categories, the first being that of the major themes and symbols, and the second being the specific songs and ritual patterns unique to any one area.

The relationship between the two categories is complex, but local material always shows specific examples of the overall patterns that occur nationally or internationally.

The international occurrence of major ballad plots and ritual patterns, dances and plays may also be considered in two ways. The most common is the ethnological and historical viewpoint, where collected material is categorised and considered as the result of great movements of early cultures across Europe (and later across the Atlantic), the different symbols and motifs being the property of loosely identified racial groups. Concurrent with this type of analysis should be the second method, which deals with the universality of the plots and patterns as presented in human consciousness. Ancient ritual plots such as *The Two Brothers** will be revealed to occur again and again in hundreds of variants widely separated geographically, and are found in the present century among both American and English folk. This astonishing recurrence may seem strange until its true meaning and value is brought to light. It could well be argued that plots of this type are the remnants of certain religious and cultural habits still reflecting themselves through thousands of years and hundreds of generations, right into the present-day descendants of primitive tribes. It should be remembered equally that the theme *regenerates* itself despite changes of language and religion, and despite vast cultural upheavals. In either case—where did the themes come from in the first place? From the human reaction to being alive, and it is not entirely necessary to point an

---

*See page 23

historical or ethnological theory to account for the persistence of certain vital symbols through time.

The value of folk symbols lies in their living quality, the fact that no amount of change in exterior culture has radically altered their potency. Modern education has destroyed the oral currency of folk songs, yet has also caused an upsurge of deep interest in folk material in the true sense of the word. All traditional material of any sort is completely unconscious and untraceable in origin—especially by those involved within it. Once a song or tale or dance or play is carried out as a conscious excercise in traditionalism, it is no longer folk material, but becomes merely folk-derived. All songs dealt with in this book are true folk material from the oral tradition.

Revived traditional practices and entertainments seem to give an enormous sense of 'rightness' when properly carried out. This rather illogical sense of satisfaction and delight that modern minds receive from reviving old songs and rituals is a significant piece of evidence. At first glance it does seem absurd that individuals living with electronic marvels of communication and entertainment, high-speed travel and chemical stimulation should even consider taking part in an activity such as Morris Dancing.* Those who do so range from respectable professional ladies and gentlemen to long-haired drop-outs. While popular entertainments today are sharply divided into carefully created and controlled consumer-groups, the participants of any 'folk' event are a completely mixed crowd. The traditional material itself appeals deeply to people of all ages and types, often in many different ways at once. The main reason for this very wide appeal is that the power of the folk racial music and symbols is not by any means dead, but still draws a response from within the regions of awareness which are far older and wiser than those inflicted by the limitations of television, school, or supermarket. It must be emphasised again and again, however, that folk culture is *not* a revolution against modern society. Although it may be thought of as such by an intellectual process and romantic wishful-thinking, 'folk' or racial consciousness is the *mainstream* from which the present culture, however repulsive and degrading, has developed and to which it will return in time.

Due to our overbalancing in destructive and unhealthy directions, we are now able to view our traditions objectively, as they begin to be systematically separated from our daily lives. Until quite recently there was no real separation between traditional culture and normal life; similarly at an earlier stage there was not any distinction between normal life and religion.

---

*Of the traditional English kind

A tradition is a racial flow of awareness presented through a set of clearly defined symbols, and will be present in all activities of any racial group that has developed it and that develops because of it.

The value of this flow of symbols is well known and often abused by politicians and commercial psychologists for sales purposes. Products of factory origin and doubtful quality are labelled 'traditional', 'country style', 'olde Worlde', and sold entirely on the escapist appeal of the advertisements rather than on any intrinsic value of the goods themselves. This immoral technique of mind-bending runs deeper than mere salesmanship. As any expert will admit, customers are affected by advertisements *despite* conscious aversion and knowledge of the tricks employed. This is simply because the symbols used act at a level of awareness that responds to certain traditional keys, no matter what conscious thought is involved. Significantly, those who take active part in traditional music and events of any sort are less likely to succumb to the power of the same symbols used for corrupt political or advertising purposes, as the energies and emotions are already being re-channelled in healthier directions.

The dangers of mass-media advertising and political jargon may seem incongruous within a study of folksong and pagan lore, but not only are they directly relevant to the subject in hand, but they are an integral and contemporary development of it. True, continuous abuse of symbols eventually feeds back causing sales resistance—but more important than loss of profit is the damage caused by such misuse. This damage is the slow erosion of the instinctive appreciation of natural life—the degradation of the beauty and the weakening of the power of our inner tradition.

And so to the songs themselves. Geographically the examples examined range from the far west of Cornwall through the whole peninsula of South-western England. One or two songs are drawn from counties bordering this region such as Gloucestershire, and from Wiltshire and the White Horse area where counties meet.

There is no geographical pattern to the evidence, as the material that the songs provide is not in any way dependent upon county divisions or earlier cultural boundaries and ancient kingdoms. The only general conclusion of this sort that may be broadly drawn is that there is more suggestion of Celtic cultures in this region, especially in the far West, than in any other part of England. Originally it was assumed that a study of this sort might indicate signs of localised remains of Celtic religion, but the accumulated evidence has pointed in a quite different direction, and shown some rather surprising links between local and national cult-patterns. To draw upon West Country songs is, in effect, to draw upon local variants of most British songs, but their particular value lies in their link with ancient ritual practices, a link shown in the symbolism of the songs themselves and in their music. A similar treatment of Eastern and North-eastern English songs would probably show a certain amount of Norse influence, but the level of symbolism found in these songs in general is deeper than that of specific religions and cults, and points to the overall pattern of images behind all magical and religious thinking.

As the evidence for this pattern is widely separated through many songs and sources, we shall be obliged to deal with some individual song examples before outlining the story that they tell.

This method may seem to be close to that of the mystery novel, but those who wish to cheat may easily refer to the sections on 'The Sacrificial Rite' and the cult of Saint George. To those unfamiliar with folk-lore, and possibly to many who think that they *are* familiar with it, direct experience of material in traditional songs themselves is the best foundation for judgement of these conclusions, and is the most convincing evidence that leads to them. Lore of this sort never opens broad and easy paths of thought, but after innumerable meanderings and branchings, leads to a simple pattern of ritual and mystical concepts, where the various separate routes merge together.

It is only fitting that the first song examined should be one that derives from a very ancient cult indeed, possibly the oldest recognisable religion in Britain of which specific elements may still be traced. As we shall find with every song, however, the symbols derive from even older faiths and unknown racial roots.

THE CUTTY WREN

(abbreviated after the second verse)

Oh where are you going? says Milder to Malder.
We may not tell you says Festle to Fose—
We're off to the wild wood, says John the Red Nose
We're off to the wild wood, says John the Red Nose.

And what will you do there? says Milder to Malder,
We may not tell you says Festle to Fose.
We'll hunt the Cutty Wren says John the Red Nose,
We'll hunt the Cutty Wren says John the Red Nose.

How will you shoot her? . . .
With bows and with arrows . . .

That will not do— . . .
What will do then? . . .
Big guns and big cannons! . . .

How will you bring her home? . . .
On four strong men's shoulders . . .

That will not do— . . .
What will do then?
Big cart and big waggons . . .

How will you cut her up? . . .
With knives and with forks.

That will not do— . . .
What will do then? . . .
Big hatchets and cleavers.

How will you cook her? . . .
In pots and in pans.

That will not do— . . .
What will do then? . . .
In a bloody great brass cauldron!

Who'll get the spare ribs? . . .
*We'll give it all to the poor.**

This curious song, which might seem to be a question-and-answer game
for children, was collected from a group of adults in Adderbury West
(Oxfordshire) in the early 1900's. They were not re-living childhood
games but were seriously carrying out an annual custom or ritual,
traditional to their home area. At first glance there might seem to be
no conceivable reason why normal country people should indulge in

---

**Note:* Texts and melodies of most song-examples are reproduced
as collected from folk-singers. Exceptions to this are *The Three
Butchers* (p. 51), *Edward* (p. 31) and *The Two Brothers,* which
combine music and words from separate sources. The examples
quoted are intended as complete models of song-types rather than
as localised fragments, but in all cases both words and music are
traditional, and have not been edited or altered.

such eccentricity as singing this song together at a certain time regularly each year; still less reason why they should thump staves on the floor of their village hall in rhythm, gathering speed to a frantic climax, and finally rush out actually to hunt a wren. The people taking part accepted this as an annual event that was 'always done' and had no logical reason for doing so. Nor was this ritual action limited to one place in particular, but it is merely one example of many similar odd events that were still practised in Britain during the early years of the century. Some are still continued to this day.

The hunting of the wren, and occasionally its crucifixion, obviously carries a greater significance than the excitement of having a rowdy good time. If there was no more to it, continual opposition by both civic and religious authority would have banned such actions centuries ago, or at least channelled the energy into more permissible outlets. The essential questions concerning the reasons for this survival, and the origin of much of the material collected, still remain a mystery.

Simple statistics show the death of traditional songs and customs in recent years. Yet the compelling quality of the material has generated such enormous interest in both lore and music that it seems impossible to keep it out of human consciousness. The questions raised by such songs as *The Cutty Wren* are not answered by modern research, but rather generate further and still further questions to which there seem to be no 'factual' answers. There is absolutely no historical focus for such material, and no accurate means of geographical analysis. A simple examination of the music and text of the songs themselves, however, reveals some startling parallels with ancient British myth and symbology, and with a religious system that is essentially pre-Christian.

The oral tradition of handing on music and lore of various sorts by word of mouth through successive generations is known to be astonishingly accurate, but this alone could not possibly explain the survival of basically Celtic or even pre-Celtic religious themes into the twentieth century. Any possible theory of secret retention and translation through the centuries of change in both society and language may be totally rejected (see *Survival of Pagan Cults*). However, the compelling chant form of the melody of *The Cutty Wren*—with its hypnotic call and response pattern—is far superior to the text that it expresses. Thus it is possible that powerful forms of music may help in the retention through time of poetry linked to them, and such a means is a more acceptable argument than is the conscious inheritance of myths.

The words of *The Cutty Wren*, however, do reveal remarkable content and pattern, worth examining in detail.

The pattern of the song is a progression of formalised questions and answers, worked by characters who have clear roles of relationship to one another. Unfortunately their identity is not at all clear and can be sought only through the way in which they act within the pattern of the song. This is, in fact, a typical ritual pattern, one common to the magical rituals of both primitive and sophisticated peoples from the aboriginal hunting rite to the modern mass communion.* Although everybody taking part knows the 'answers' to the questions, the real content lies in the accumulation of riddles created by the pattern of the ritual. The drawn-out progression and the rhythm and chant elements are typical means of focussing awareness on the matter in hand, widely used for many purposes today from education to formal liturgy, not to mention television commercials and popular music. The close similarity between the construction of many folksongs and liturgical chants is significant, though usually ignored. One might begin to suspect that some of these songs *are* liturgical chants or ritual music, no matter how corrupt or altered the form. The similarity discovered is *not* with the hymn-singing or congregational music of the present day or even recent centuries, but with much earlier forms. It cannot be seriously argued that folksong is derived from the influence of early Church music. There is, however, a mass of evidence that plainsong modes were naturally developed from the types of scale and song used by the common people.

The symbolism of *The Cutty Wren* bears a close relationship to various forms of mythological, religious and mystical modes of thought. Add to the powerful vehicle of the music the drive of these basic racial symbols, and we may discover the secret of survival through all changes of language and custom. As the material itself is from simple levels of awareness that are essentially non-verbal, the changes through time that would seem to pose an historical problem may not be of such significance after all. This is not to suggest an esoteric or cult origin that causes the songs to re-occur, but rather the basic reality of crude symbols that are consistent with an agricultural society. Such a way of life existed in Britain until the early years of this century, and in a few regions still survives.

The formalised characters of *The Cutty Wren* plot challenge and respond to each other. Their purpose is to hunt the Cutty (little) Wren, a common small bird, once depicted on the British farthing coin. This bird, it seems, cannot simply be chased and caught—mere bows and arrows are insufficient—big guns and big cannons are needed; carts and wagons will be necessary to bring it home, and hatchets and cleavers to cut her up. The repeated emphasis on something small that is also very great is a common type of mystical utterance or way of

---

*See also song appendix, *Hymn of Jesus*.

thinking, but obviously such a comparison alone is not enough to suggest that the song might be 'religious'. The final fate of this tiny bird is that it can be cooked and utilised to feed the poor. It has been suggested from this conclusion that the song is political, but internal evidence proves that it is religious. Curiously, out of the thousands of political broadsheets and songs in pamphlets that were sold or distributed and sung popularly around the country during the past 400 years, very few have survived within the folk tradition. For every one known political song collected there are scores of romances, and dozens of ballads and songs showing ancient ritual content, or early forms of mythology.

The crucifying of the hunted wren (once actually carried out by country folk), is unlikely to be a reference to the fate wished on the capitalist landlord, but *is* quite possibly a direct link with the typical sacrificial forms of religion known to use the cross as a symbol, including Christianity. *The Cutty Wren* may have been used at political gatherings, but it certainly did not originate at one.

The wren is often known to be a symbol for the King,* a concept well represented in various songs and rituals that relate to the basic 'Cutty Wren' theme. Folk-lore of the wren is abundant, and it is usually accepted that the wren-king is likely to be a form of symbolism or substitution for the human sacrificial victim. In the Christian ritual a substitution was also made for the body and blood, and the relationship of the symbology is very clear on certain points. The killing of the wren in folk custom was supposed to bring fertility to the fields and good luck to everyone, and a revealing key is the cooking and eating of it, in a brass cauldron.

The division of the sacrifice to feed many people, or to bring many people salvation, is well represented in religious thought and legend. The spare-rib alone, of the wren, will feed the poor, after the workers of the ritual killing and cutting and cooking have taken their share.† The cooking in a 'by our Lady' brass cauldron bears a close resemblance to certain Celtic myths concerning the magical cauldron of Kerridwen, the ancient British mother-goddess, and the British version of the Harrying of Hell. In this, the spoils are not souls, as in the Christian myth, but an inexhaustable cauldron is included.

The cauldron of Kerridwen was the source of immortality and divine wisdom, and the customary promise of salvation through the death of a saviour. If we remember that the ritual death of certain individuals was a common practice of salvation and god-seeking, not

---

*See Frazer, *The Golden Bough*.
†See Gospel according to St. Mark, chapter 8.

by any means unique to the Christian faith, we shall see that *The Cutty Wren* is concerned with such practices.

The myth of the Cauldron has various aspects, but all revert to a simple relation of concepts. The Goddess Kerridwen is a Welsh aspect of the ancient Mother Goddess, who took various shapes depending upon her function (see *The Two Magicians*, p. 40). The legend tells how she brewed a magical concoction in a cauldron, the result of which was wisdom and immortality. Another tale gives the amazing story of a descent to the Underworld in search of a magical cauldron, source of immortality and wisdom. In Ireland the invading Tuatha de Dannann brought four magical objects with them, the spear of Lugh (Light) which ensured victory, the sword of Nuadha, which was inescapable, the stone of Fal which identified true kings by shrieking, and the inexhaustable cauldron of the Daghda. This legendary theme shows the four magical weapons used in all Western ritual—the Sword, Rod, Cup (cauldron), and Shield. These same talismans or implements were passed on through time until the sword became the property of Saint George, the Lance that of Saint Michael, the cauldron became the Holy Grail, and the Stone appears in tradition as 'Corpus Christi' (see song appendix, *Down in Yon Forest*).

The particular appearance of the cauldron in our folksong is strictly apposite to its theme. The wren was the totem symbol for the Celtic god Bran, who probably derives from an even earlier source (see Lewis Spence). He was an oracular hero, a being who linked the outer world with the Underworld. His head may still be seen upon remains of a Roman-Celtic temple in Bath, the ancient city of *Aquae Sulis*. His hair and beard and long moustaches are typically Celtic, and he has a minute pair of wings which shows his identity with the local cult hero, Bladud, who was a British 'Icarus' figure. He is supported not only by two typical Roman or borrowed Greek figures, but also by Owls, the totem-bird of the infernal Goddess. (Regrettably, classically obsessed early archaeologists termed this figure 'a curious male Medusa', being unable to see nearer home than the invading Romans. Although this error is now known, the tourist trade is too profitable to dare confuse visitors with the truth).

Bran's head, which in legend uttered prophecies after being separated from his body, was not at *Aquae Sulis* by accident. The hot springs and caves were the centre of an oracular death-cult, the basic form of British religion, where a seeress sat over the steaming heady waters and linked her mind to that of the cult hero, who was supposed to be in the Underworld.* The dark steaming cave from which the waters flowed

---

*Archaeological, legendary and historic evidence all suggest this conclusion.

Not an unusual male Medusa, as we are often led to believe, but the head of a Celtic deity, probably Bran. (Reproduced by courtesy of The Pitman Press, who use this drawing as their house symbol.)

was a local manifestation of the Cauldron of Kerridwen, for Sulis, the goddess presiding over the waters, was a goddess of pigs ('Suilis' means a swine, pig or sow), and the totem beast of the goddess Kerridwen was the Sow.

The most primitive forms of religion are death and ancestor cults, where ghosts or spirits are supposed to advise from their superior vantage-point. The Cauldron is typically cross-identified with the Underworld itself, both the 'subconscious' of modern psychological theory and the Abyss of mysticism. Christs' Harrowing of Hell is seldom mentioned today, but it played an important role in early Christianity, as it followed directly from the worship of cults such as that of Bran and his classical and Eastern counterparts. As cultures evolved, the actual human sacrifice was replaced by various substitutes: within living memory, the Oxfordshire folk and people of the White Horse Vale were still singing the song of this substitution sacrifice . . ..

Whatever the personal beliefs of the people working folk-ritual in the twentieth century, these beliefs did not seem to conflict with the ceremony. It is probable the link was established intellectually and comfortably by those who enacted the ritual through succeeding generations. The functions of the characters of *The Cutty Wren* are those of a principal officer (John the Red Nose)—who declares all final solutions and statements—and two teams of liturgists, Milder & Malder, and Festle & Fose. These two teams or choirs create the question-and-negation pattern which the principal officer grandly solves at the end of each verse.

The survival of ancient lore in folksongs and rituals is due to a combination of various factors. The accuracy and retention of the oral tradition need not be totally ignored, but perhaps the idea of a racial memory of tradition would be a better means of explaining the survival of myths. One vital factor is the agricultural way of life. These songs were usually collected from rural communities, and such material is not found or practised in modern cities. The sacrificing of the wren was supposed to bring fertility. This would be a natural part of the life-cycle, where death leads to new birth through the ceaseless round of the seasons. There is no dark ancient religious secret involved here, but simply the epitomising of the processes by which the rural community lived. The line of survival of racial myths could, poetically speaking, come out of the land itself, through the humans who live upon it. The link with later sophisticated religious concepts is hardly surprising when we consider that these concepts grew naturally out of the roots of human existence.

The natural element is broken and diffused by intellectual organisation, as it depends upon unconscious use. Early church music and ritual was gradually intellectualised to a fine degree, often changing with the wind of political expediency, but the folk-patterns from which it all evolved carried on unbroken. Modern education has succeeded in destroying for most people the essentially pagan life-relationship that the greatest minds of the Christian Church could not touch.

The musical content of ritual songs is a special study of its own right (see 'Musical Considerations', p. 93), but certain vital points are worth mentioning in connection with *The Cutty Wren*. As we have seen, the performance is carried out in a manner similar to liturgical practice, with calls and responses in ordered pattern. While this question-and-answer sequence is common to many ritual songs in the tradition, the shape of the melody itself is similar in many ways to certain aspects of plainsong, though it has a wilder and freer flow and range of notes. These were precisely the qualities that early authorities formally banned in an attempt to control the reactions of the congregation during church services.

The rhythm is a throbbing three-fold beat, which was a rule—sometimes attributed to the symbolism of the Holy Trinity—laid down very strictly for early church music. Not surprisingly we find that the ancient British religion was based on a three-fold system also. Again, we must grow beyond the argument of 'who-stole-what-from-whom' and see proof of a natural continuity of symbolism expressed through the music and song of ordinary people.

The symbolic content of the song remains despite the corruption or adaptation of the words for more modern use. The process of conscious and unconscious translation of songs is a fascinating one . . . and holds a great deal more than any of the old jokes about passing messages along a line of people. The impact and vitality of *The Cutty Wren* is enormous. Its power is striking to the modern listener, no matter how far removed he is from the life-cycle which it represents.

Quite possibly the attraction of such material for modern scholars and musicians is not primarily in the depth of curious lore that it holds, but in the life forces from which it grows. In the 'pagan' songs we can feel the essential flow of life expressing itself directly, a quality long departed from most formal religious music. There is no dogma or philosophy remaining to tie the mind, and we are free to respond naturally to the impulse of the rituals and songs themselves.

The fragment of ritual surviving in *The Cutty Wren*, in its various English versions, stops short with the death and eating of the victim. It does not continue the tale, as do the Irish legends, with the magical revival and rebirth, although the wren-hunt was still associated with the growth of crops.

To continue the story we must look to another song altogether, which at first sight appears to have no ritual elements at all, as it belongs to that curious group of songs usually classified as 'narrative ballads'. With this song we not only continue the story, but add an important character, and incidentally the influence of a culture which overran and absorbed that of Bran's people.

This does not mean that there is a historical progression to the story, for we shall see that the theme itself appears in many forms in many lands, and it is important not to fall into the trap of regarding mythical history as a logical progression connected to events such as wars, tribal emigrations or the rise and fall of civilisations. Specific aspects of myths may be atrributed to certain cultures by way of making valuable reference-points, but there are no hard-and-fast definitions, and certainly no last word or authoritative sources.

THE TWO BROTHERS

It's of two brothers going to the school
a going to the very same school
and one of them unto the other one said,
can you throw a ball?

Oh I can neither throw a stone,
nor can I throw a ball,
but if you go down to the merry greenwoods
I'll throw you a wrestling fall.

Oh they went down to the merry greenwoods
beneath a struggling moon,
and a penknife fell from out John's pocket
and gave him his dead wound.

What will you tell my mother dear
this night when you come home?
I'll tell her that you've gone to the western woods
a-learning the hounds to run.

What will you tell my father dear
this night when you come home?
I'll tell him that you've gone to the foreign school
your letters for to learn.

What will you tell my true love dear
this night when you come home?
I'll tell her that you're dead and in your grave,
where the small birds weep and mourn.

But when young Suzy heard of this,
she charmed the birds from out their nests,
she charmed young John all out of his grave
where he was all at rest.

This very widespread ballad is one of the essential myths of the British people. A root-theme of all Western mythology and religion, it may be traced back to actual ritual practice. The story is clearly found in Celtic and pre-Celtic myth and lore, in classical mythology, and in ancient Egyptian and Eastern religious allegory.

The plot is very simple, one brother kills another in competition for a woman. The murdered man is then brought back to life by his true love. The pattern is one of Life-Death-Resurrection, found in all religious thinking from the earliest and crudest nature-worship to the refined intellectual speculations of theology. No story could be simpler, yet none contains such a wealth of meaning. Entire religions and vast empires have grown and fallen through manifestations of this one myth as dogma. Yet the folk-theme has remained constant to the elements of the act, which derives from the worship of a Mother-Lover-Goddess in whose control all life, and all death, were held.

A clear link connects this ballad with the early ritual practice of the

Sacred King and his Tanist Brother and Successor.* Although actual practices in specific times and places are known to have varied enormously, the general pattern was this: at a certain time of the year, one chosen man superseded the present 'king' usually by killing him. The victim represented the light part or waxing year, his successor the dark season, or waning year. The story never ends, for the goddess brings the light-brother back to life in the spring, at the end of the dark-brother's reign.

These two brothers have fought their way through human consciousness during the entire history of man's existence. The list of their names (apart from Jack and John as the ballads always call them) is long indeed: Horus and Set, Cain and Abel, Beli and Bran, Balin and Balan, the pattern is the same. Light and dark, good and evil, Winter and Summer, positive and negative, Michael and Lucifer, Christ and Satan, life and death—all forms of metaphysical pairing of opposites are extensions of the Two Brothers. The resolving element in this perpetual struggle is the Goddess who restores, or Life Power itself.

As is usual in folksong, we come across the root of the myth in a direct form, stripped of all historical or philosophical accumulations. The starkness and reality of folksongs is deceptively simple, for all extra material has been discarded, yet the powerful images are never weakened or lost. An examination of the text shows some recognisable traces of early ritual and mythical themes associated with human sacrifice. The folk memory works as an unconscious store of power images, rather than a racial tape-recorder and translator. The battle of the brothers retains only slight traces of the religions that have grown up around it, and although the folk-singer sings it as an actual occurrence it makes obvious nonsense as a murder plot. The emblems of pre-Christian belief are clear to see, and only in this fashion can the ballad become meaningful. If the life-symbols were not present the song would have disappeared long ago.

Most variants involve a battle by wrestling, which seems to turn into accidental death by stabbing. Others rely more simply on direct stabbing:

> 'you're not the one that Suzy loves,
> and here I swear I'll take your life,
> And he stabbed him through his gentle heart
> with his long-daggered knife.'

Curiously, the practice of wrestling has a religious significance, connected with the practice of ritually maiming the Sacred King to mark

---

*See Graves, Frazer, etc.

him as being set aside. The best known example of this is the story of
Jacob wrestling with the Angel. This theme lasted right through into
the Grail romances, with the story of the maimed Fisher King. (See
Corpus Christi Carol or *Down in Yon Forest* p. 122.)

The folk ballads nearly all insist on wrestling, though the death is
by stabbing. Possibly two practices have been condensed into one, the
ritual maiming and stabbing to death would normally have been quite
distinct events, separated by at least a year if not a longer period of
time. One could consider the reference to the brothers fighting beneath
a 'wrestling' or 'struggling' moon to imply that there was a definite
right time for this activity. It should be noted that folk ballads seldom
colour their plots with metaphor, and where this process occurs it is
usually of a very specific nature, and not a poetical conceit. We do
know that early people carefully calculated and observed the celestial
patterns. The ritual Sacrifice was supposed to have been made when
Sun and Moon were equal in the sky, approximately every eight years.

After the death wound comes a ritual question-and-answer sequence,
in this case so vital that some variants have lost the initial argument
verses, and get straight down to the ritual questions and the revival of
the dead man by his true love. Logically this makes no sense at all,
but the illogical mythical selection that a group-consciousness makes
always seems to retain the most important elements without ascribing
any intellectual interpretation. Some folk-singers, when asked about
ballads of this sort, would give the matter some thought and explain
it as a true story . . . but it happened some years ago, not far from here.
This kind of reply or statement is familiar to most folk-song collectors.
Usually all living relatives of the hero or heroine are dead, and no-one
can remember exactly when or where it was . . . but it is true all the
same.

Depending upon the variant of the song, the questions are sometimes
put by one brother, sometimes by the other. If the original pattern was
that of the living man asking questions of the dying one—

> 'What will I tell my mother dear,
> this night when I get home?'

—we may have a hint of the slayer asking the victim for prophetic
words or signs, a common ancient practice still maintained today in the
supersitition that man's dying word must be upheld. This practice is
also still found in primitive forms of worship such as animal sacrifice
for augury or in spiritualism. If the formal questions are asked by the
victim, the answers become a form of identifying, or other-world
instruction, as found in the ancient Mysteries mentioned in much
classical literature.

In this particular plot the pieces of the story are scattered through several variants, and no one text collected from oral tradition holds every element. The general order of the questions is that of Father and Mother first, with True Love always the final dramatic question. The family question-and-answer ritual is found in several ballads that concern murder, and may suggest that certain ballads, such as *Lord Randall* (where a man is poisoned by his lover and his mother arrives at the revelation by careful questioning) may have lost pagan significance, but could be of ritual origin.

Several interesting Celtic links are shown in collected verses of *The Two Brothers*, scattering throughout versions noted down from oral tradition. The study of folksong and lore is essentially spread through a large number of examples of any one theme, and even further through the many examples of related themes. The process should be one of synthesis, but only in the light of a majority of one plot or motif, using the more colourful variants to illuminate certain aspects of more common versions.

It should be emphasised that there is never a *correct* version of any folksong, only variants sung by folk-singers. Some variants are more 'right' than others, but any standards are arbitrary as there is no authority other than statistics to refer to. Sometimes it is not possible to find even the basic narrative action of a ballad, especially in the well-known cases where the plot has been reduced to a few verses of riddle or romance which live on after the original story has been forgotten. Loss of narrative, however, dose not apply as much to the ancient or ritual ballads as to the broadside or popular plots. This implies that the power of the ancient ballads lies in the magical material of which they are made, and such stuff is not easily whittled away, because of its essential starkness and strength. How can basic life-keys be forgotten or trimmed? They are the symbols of human existence that grow within our consciousness; though the language of expression may alter, the basic images are true and timeless.

Some variants of *The Two Brothers* show a clear implication of human sacrifice:

> 'Will you go to the rolling of the stones
> The throwing of the ball
> And will you go to see little Suzy
> Dance among them all?
>
> Will you drink of the blood
> The white wine and the red,
> And will you go to see little Suzy
> When that I am dead?'

This first immediately reminds us of a ritual choosing by lot, but may have an even more important significance. If the famous myth of Paris is really a misrepresentation of the Goddess giving the apple of immortality to the Hero (see Robert Graves, *White Goddess*), then we find the same concept embodied in this folk-verse. In either case we have a viable ritual context connected with the pattern of the myth. The phrase 'rolling of the stones' is reminiscent of the countryman's stories about the stones that roll and dance round in circles at night. This widespread folk-tale, plus the connected moral story about attending stones that once were dancers (petrified for daring to profane the Christian Sabbath), still links the ancient sites with the worship of the past. Possibly traces of this worship carried through in some areas until quite recently, though this does not imply a connection with the popular suburban cults of 'witchcraft' that have flourished since the repeal of the Witchcraft Act in the 1950s.

The drinking of the blood needs no skill in interpretation. In the earliest form of the eucharistic rite the victim was literally dismembered and eaten. This practice was common throughout the ancient world at specific places and times of the year, even after the Roman legislation introduced Emperor worship with a ban on life-sacrifices other than animals. The great value of the revelation that later developed into Christianity was that it was a return to powerful and familiar forms of worship. This fact is easily missed due to deliberate suppression of evidence and information, but the Christian faith worked not because of its unique quality but because of its regression to an ancient pattern inhibited by the state-worship of political gods. The form of the new revelation, however, was unique, for the victim (after his death was seen to be inevitable) substituted bread and wine for body and blood. The reason for the widespread acceptance of Christian practice was its pagan quality, its connection with the sacrificial rites known throughout the Western world. It grew in popularity not because it was *new*, but because it was a revolutionary means of returning to the ancient faith in defiance of state worship.

The verse dealing with the running of the hounds in the Western woods links the ballad with the ancient myth of the kings' soul being seen as a deer, pursued into the West by the Hounds of Hell. Dogs have always been the guardians of the underworld, and the Gabriel hounds pursued souls well into the present century in popular superstition.

The ritual killing ends in rebirth—resurrection—in both the Christian and pre-Christian myths.

> 'Suzy charmed the birds from their nests
> And the fish from out the bay,

> She charmed young John all out of his grave
> And all in his arms did lay.

or

> She's wept and mourned right bitterly
> She's wept from door to door
> And she's wept him all out of his very own grave
> Till rest he could get no more'

In many versions it is not Suzy's weeping, but her singing and her harping, or in one obviously lapsed text from the USA, her hopping all over his grave! The magic of music brings the dead back to life, charms the birds from their nests, wins the fish from the bay. Poetically she sings the song of life, and all living things respond to her music, including her chosen dead lover. The continual ancient association of music with divine power is an involved and fascinating subject, stretching from primitive chants and mimic noises for the most basic tribal rites to the sophisticated soothing and uplifting beauty of plainsong. Music has always been the power of the Divine ones, so one would naturally expect that the Goddess revives her lover with a song.

In most examples the ballad ends with the resurrection verse, but occasionally there is an addition of a well-known verse usually connected with 'the Unquiet Grave' or 'Sweet William's Ghost':

> 'What do you want with me Suzy
> What do you want with me?
> 'One kiss one kiss from your clay cold lips
> then get you back to your grave.'

These later additions, which are in a minority, draw upon the grief-motive of revival rather than the magical theme. It was popularly believed that excessive grief troubles the dead and causes them to return to the world of the living to complain that their after-life sleep is being disturbed. This theme has very little direct connection with the ritual aspect of *The Two Brothers* and may be regarded as a rationalisation of the true plot.

In a few variants of the ballad we find a verse dealing with the idea that the victim's wound cannot be staunched. In some versions his brother tries to wash and bind the wound but the more he washes it, the more it bleeds.* The bleeding of wounds, especially upon corpses, was considered to be evidence that the murderer was near. This common

---

*See Genesis chapter 4, verses 1–16.

belief may be mirrored here, but it is unlikely that the verses refer to the original concept from which various superstitious and religious ideas have developed. We may have an implication, in this case, of the ever-bleeding wounds of the sacrificial victim. This belief is found in the Grail legends, and obviously in Christian dogma. The shedding of the Sacred Kings' blood was for all his people, later adapted into a sin-punishment obsession by decree.

Originally the belief may have been that the sharing of the victim's blood brought a trace of divinity to those who partook of it. More simply, the primitive rite of drinking blood was supposed to put as many people as possible into communion with his departing spirit. Before examining the general order of the Sacred Victim ritual, another ballad, closely linked with *The Two Brothers*, should be analysed.

The link between *Edward* and *The Two Brothers* is obvious: one story relates the actual drama of the murder, while the other deals with the questioning of the murderer after he returned home. In some ballads the two stories are run together as one song—but more often they occur as separate dramatic events. It is impossible to state whether the two stories were originally linked, or if folk-singers simply identified the tales with each other; certainly there is a logical connection between the two. It is possible to suggest that some of the ancient ballads form a ritual song-story cycle, which may have been part of a religious mystery such as the famous Mystery Plays performed in medieval times. It should always be remembered that most people were illiterate until quite recently. The farther back in time, the more the oral tradition was essential. As it was necessary to put the Biblical stories into drama for the English peasant, so would his ancestors have received their public religious exposition in the form of song and drama. Surviving pagan rites such as the Padstow May Song and Dance show quite clearly that worship was not separated from the seasons of the year or from everyday life. This is a matter easily forgotten by modern minds—that our ancestors did not experience the false separation between 'religion' and 'real life' that is universal today. All life-activities were 'religious' because all living was part of the pattern of Life. Only when religion dies does it become a separate compartment of experience disassociated from day-to-day activity.

This is not to suggest that all apparently magical songs from the British tradition are or were originally part of one enormous scheme of cult-lore. This would be as absurd as suggesting that all hymns and church-services still in use are similarly co-ordinated.

The many ritual songs, mummers' plays, dances and other genuine folk-events found all over Britain show a mixture of local and universal practice. Certain dances, for example, were strictly localised. The sword-dancing of the North shows some quite clear ritual weaving-patterns allied to Cosmic creation myths, but we find no trace of this in the West Country. Many ballads express ancient beliefs, but often they are beliefs that contradict each other. The spectrum of myth and lore is not one that can be accurately fixed in time: ancient and modern beliefs are sometimes found side by side, and ballad variants will occasionally provide significant changes of plot that show a change of belief at some untraceable date. The grief-resurrection pattern of *The Two Brothers*, as opposed to the life-resurrection pattern, is a good example of this. The grief-concept suggests a period when belief has slowed into superstition and the mythical quality begins to have a logical explanation tagged on to it. The advent of new formal faiths of religion or materialism does not destroy the old images, they merely return to the regions of symbolism within the folk memory.

EDWARD

(abbreviated after the first verse)

How come that blood upon your sword?
my son come tell to me.
It is the blood of my little greyhound dog
that would not run for me.

O a greyhound's blood was ne'er so clear . . .
It is the blood of my grey mare,
she would not ride for me.

O but a grey mare's blood was ne'er so clear . . .
O it is the blood of my dear little brother
who rode away with me.

What did you two fall out about? . . .
It was that he plucked up a little hazel bush
that should have grown up into a tree.

The ballad *Edward* is an excellent piece of dramatic suspense. The entire plot is revealed through a question-and-answer sequence from beginning to end, with no simple narrative at all. As soon as the murder has come out—after an interesting series in which the victims become larger in size and greater in life-value—the fulcrum of the action is the following verse:

> And what did you two fall out about?
> My son come tell to me
> It was that he plucked up a little hazel bush
> That should have become a tree.

This seemingly bizarre reason for a murder gives a clue to the ritual nature of the song. The hazel is always known as the sacred tree of wisdom in Irish mythology, and to uproot a hazel at one time was punishable by death. If one accepts Graves' calendar of the Trees, as restored from ancient poems and alphabet lore, the Hazel tree comes at the turning of the year. If this was indeed the case, then the murder was carried out when the light part of the year turned into the dark part. The little hazel-bush may represent the spirit or soul of the victim.

The cutting of the hazel-bush or other tree, found in variants of this ballad, has a direct link with Celtic religion. Lucan (1st Century A.D.) and a later commentator (*De Bello Civilii* 1,444–6) mentions a Gaulish deity called Esus 'of the barbarous altars'. Victims sacrificed to this god were said to have been hung from trees, and ritually wounded. This is immediately suggestive of JESUS who underwent similar ritual—or of ODIN who hung upon the windy World Tree for nine days and nights.

A relief carving, dated somewhere between A.D. 14 and 37, was found in 1711 under the choir of Notre Dame Cathedral. It shows a crude figure entitled ESUS cutting down a little tree. Whatever the original myth of this and similar beliefs may have been, the folksong suggests that it was part of the death-resurrection theme, as do the connected Norse and Semitic myths of Tree-Sacrifice. It is common for the primitive soul to be identified with a tree and for a tree to be the nature-symbol of a god or goddess. Symbolically the tree is the Tree of Life, a comprehensive glyph which is found in songs such as *The Keys of Heaven* or 'Dilly Song' examined later.

The 'penances' which the victim imposes upon himself are interesting. The bottomless boat is the Ark (not necessarily of Noah) or sacred vessel in which the hero sets out upon the ocean of the unknown. It reminds us of the Druidic rite that involved a ritual journey across the foam in a magical boat (see Lewis Spence). It also links with many stories of the Divine Child who was found floating in a vessel upon ocean or river. The verse could well read that the murderer's 'punishment' was to become reborn again as a victim from the waters of the Mother-Deep. The hero floating in an ark can be found in ancient Egyptian mythology and included Noah, Moses, Herakles, Taliesin and many others. Later we shall see that this illustrious list of heroes includes Saint George.

The final verse is a powerful piece of poetry. There is a general category of folk-lyrics of a slightly riddling nature, which define usually impossible events, conditions or tasks. These verses are actually of two sorts.

The first is that of lyrical or romantic sentiment—

> 'When the fishes do fly
> And the seas run dry,
> Oh its then you will marry I'

These romantic protestations form an important part of folk-lyrics, but are quite distinct from another form of riddling, which is magical in origin, and in content.

The impossible condition is always the sign of ritual or magical battle or action. Perhaps the best example of this is the popular folksong *Parsley Sage Rosemary and Thyme* or *The Elfin Knight*.

Formerly such questions and answers were found in ritual use as has been suggested by *The Cutty Wren*. The mythology of life and death is greatly concerned with riddles and magical questions—the prize is usually eternal life and the penalty death and rebirth. The stylised rites of the Freemasons are good examples of magical questions and answers, even though they no longer have any religious impetus.

The problem with poetic statements of the impossible is that they have more than one level of meaning and are, in fact, open ways through which meaning can pass at will. The Sun and Moon verse may imply again the importance of celestial phenomena in ancient religious rites—the Sacred King was appointed to die when the Sun and Moon were equal in the sky . . . but when was he appointed to come back again? The divine child who was sought by the 'Three Wise Men' was heralded by a star, and for countless centuries man has watched and calculated the motions of the stars and planets.

It is the seemingly impossible quality that flows through all mythic statements that causes consciousness to pause, and perhaps alter its point of view. The significance of such curious lines and odd actions, apparently meaningless in themselves, is that they can link individual awareness with wider fields of consciousness, usually inaccessible in ordinary thinking. This does not imply telepathy or clairvoyance, but simply the changing of focus from individual limitations to wider cycles in time and space. This process will be familiar to those who have examined 'Zen' poetry—without realising that such mind-bending verses were used in Britain for thousands of years, being a Druidic talent of excellence. The remaining remnants of grand Bardic conundrums are to be found in fragments of late Welsh and Irish poetry, Celtic myth and lore, and also in common-or-garden folksongs.

The connection between *Edward* and *The Two Brothers* cannot be analysed specifically. They are simple survivors of two aspects of the same mythical plot and do not link logically in terms of factual examination (Why hazel and not true love? Why doesn't the brother in *Edward* use the verse he has prepared in *The Two Brothers* as excuses? Is it because he has been caught out by verse one?). Simple logic does not apply to the ballads, one has to travel-forwards-while-always-looking-behind, with a dog as guide. This is the way of the deer-soul, of course, as the King is pursued by the Hounds of the Other World. In folk-lore Gabriel brings not only the annunciation—but also the way of death (see section on 'Dilly Song' p. 73).

The Sacrificial Rite

The general outline of the rites of human sacrifice and Divine Kingship has been covered very thoroughly by many reference-works on myth and anthropology. Despite this extensive coverage, it is worth re-examining the ritual that is hinted at in many folksongs, folk-tales and ceremonies. References to the act are widely scattered through numerous books, articles and documents ranging from detailed scholarship to sensational journalism—yet a fresh assessment in the present context may shed some light on this seemingly dark and barbaric practice.

The actual details of the rites of human sacrifice in pagan times vary enormously—yet the basic concepts and methods of operation are clear and simple. At certain pre-determined times, selected individuals were killed by specific means. These 'sacred kings' lived a closely ordered life, with privileges and restraints outside normal behaviour and rules. In each case, the dying victim was replaced by a chosen heir, often his murderer, who in turn died an unnatural death when his time came. It is clear that certain forms of the rite involved actual eating of the flesh and drinking the blood of the victim. The selection of the victim was at times determined by controlled breeding among chosen women, a caste of priestesses.

Such facts are found in early myths and classical references, well documented and interpreted by many scholars. The immensely varied and colourful details of this pattern of behaviour have generated an immense amount of literature and special study.

After the briefest exploration into this ancient ritual and belief one question occurs to the modern mind, but it is precisely this that most studies leave unanswered. Why did people worship in this fashion?

If it is accepted that human beings are prompted by utterly absurd, irrational, fear-driven impulses, then we are compelled to admit that the entire fabric of early societies was always supported by ignorance and terror. We must therefore concede that modern society is at last approaching true enlightenment as it abandons ancient superstition in favour of computerised consumer units. Such an outlook leaves our rather difficult question unsolved, as it is by no means sufficient to suggest that all known societies and civilisations of the past were un-reasonable and ignorant, although they did lack mechanical hardware. Many of the powerful minds that we have record of, and no doubt those we do not know of, would regard our civilisation as the epitome of barbarism—a structure based upon the dehumanising of the individual without any overall meaning or pattern other than dubious tokens of profit.

The origins of the sacrificial rite are remarkably simple. Living things seemed to run in a cycle from birth through to death, and back to birth again. This cycle of life is clearly expressed again and again in folksong and myth—the seasons of the year turning round, and life reappearing out of death. This vision of a life-cycle is not merely founded upon a primitive fear of death, it is based upon empirical observation, a concept of the facts of nature. The key to this type of awareness expressed in myth and religion is that life is impersonal, not anti-personal, and pagan faiths relate or attempt to relate to Life, rather than to individual lives. The culmination of this concept is found in the human sacrifice pattern, around which developed a complex system of metaphysical beliefs and practices.

It was believed that as plants, animals and other life-forms passed into the earth at death, and were eventually reborn afresh, so did mankind. Life passed into another world after physical death, a world which formed the link between Winter and Spring. This Other-world was under the protection of the Earth Mother, as all living things were observed to die into the earth, and to spring up from it. The Earth Mother, therefore, was worshipped as a divine being from whom all food, life and death were seen to come. As conceptual ability developed, the life-link became aspected as the various goddesses, gods and powers that make up the pagan pantheon. The naivety of this development does not entirely imply ignorance—for when we consider today the primal forces of nuclear physics, or the measureless depths of space-time, we are effectively contemplating the 'All Father' or the 'Great Mother'.

The sacrificial victim was a *willing contributor* to the pattern of life. By his voluntary death he went consciously to the Other-world, and while there he was to attempt to learn from the Mother, and to relay her wisdom back to his people. By performing a willed ritual cycle of deaths and rebirths, the pagan peoples aspired to harmonise with and contribute to the greater life-cycles that they felt evident around them. The deaths and ritual conceptions were timed according to careful observation of the stars and planets, assimilated through many lifetimes of watching and calculating.

When the Star, Sun and Moon paths were in line, a willing Traveller could go to, or come from, the Other-world.

An important factor was the Sybil, Priestess or Seeress. She was not merely an intoxicated or euphoric woman who mumbled enigmatic riddles, but was supposed to be a medium for the communications of the Sacred King or hero in the Other-world. When he went there, with questions to ask or contacts to establish, she was the two-way link, still living *here*. This process was usually allowed to continue for a specific time or sun-cycle, by the end of which the victim lost contact, or was freed from his obligation, and a fresh phase of sacrifice was initiated with a new Sacred King.

A sophisticated development of the concept was that as the dedicated special souls of the sacred kings evolved through their wisdom of the Other-world, so they would choose to re-incarnate, starting a fresh cycle to aid their own people. Specific incarnation rites were carried out to this end, and the chaste nun is the descendant of the sacred priestesses of the Goddess, who bred specifically to give birth to a divine being. Gradually the advanced concept of the incarnation of a divinely-evolved being grew out of this ritual theory.

Anyone vaguely familiar with Christianity will see certain links with the ancient cults, and realise that Christian monastic practice was not a fresh institution but a direct descendant of the earlier sacred king and 'virgin' priestess colleges. The true reasons for the ancient faith could never be answered by any of the Christian cults, least of all the Roman Church, without frankly admitting that such cults merely extended an incredibly ancient faith, and re-established a new phase of the powerful Human-Life, All-Life relationship formed by ritual sacrifice. The concept of incarnate divinity was never the unique property of Christianity, and the early attempts to annexe and capitalise on 'spiritual power' have caused little else than disaster throughout Christian history.

The role of Sacred King was much sought after, and was never that of a forced or unwilling victim. Undoubtedly unwilling ritual murders were, and possibly are, carried out, but these do not connect with the ancient life rituals, and represent a more sinister or anti-evolutionary set of ideas. The sacred victims and the priests and priestesses of the ancient deities were highly honoured and revered people, in whom real faith in power was vested by the ordinary people. Whether this honour and faith was justified or not is a matter of individual judgement, but the ancient mediators were considered to be *working* links with Divinity, and not theorists or powerless social workers.

The Other-world journey is clearly described in many native British myths, fairy-tales and heroic poems. This travelling to 'Paradise' such as was undertaken by the Irish Heroes, the Welsh Arthur, the Scots Thomas the Rhymour and many others, was achieved traditionally in two ways. Firstly, the beneficial Other-world, the Blessed Isles, Avalon, or the Apple Orchard, the Land of Eternal Youth, could be revealed. In the revelation, the chosen one is translated immediately to the wonderful realms direct from the ordinary world, usually by fairies or magical beings. Secondly, a mortal man may *win* his way to Paradise, by passing tests of travel and travail through the intervening realms or worlds or planes of the Underworld. The quest of Arthur for the cauldron in the Old Welsh poem *Preiddeu Annwn* (The Spoils of Annwn) shows this journey and battle, as does the Scots ballad of Thomas Rhymour, but with less heroic emphasis. The classical parallel is to be found in the Mysteries which existed solely to instruct the initiate how to pass through the infernal or intervening realms to reach the land of the immortals.

The entire set of concepts reappears in the stories of the romantic Arthur and his Round Table. Sir Galahad has the Grail (once upon a time the Cauldron) *revealed* to him by reason of his own pure nature . . . yet he was the product of an unwitting physical liaison. This is exactly the ancient practice being echoed, whereby a Divine Child of unknown father or mother, or at least with some mystery about his conception, later becomes a Saviour. The practice was again revived, with certain specific changes, in the Order of the Garter, which links closely with the traditional May Day fertility rites. Even today these folk-rituals are licentious, but not as freely and openly practised as in years past.

Once the worship theme of our ancestors has been considered, we cannot miss recognising its appearance in many many folksongs and tales. This type of worship apparently was conscious in the minds of everyone, at least as recently as the perpetuation of the Order of the Garter, and until the present century in folk practice.

The line runs from a deeply rooted life-death cult which must have originated in primitive hunting society, through a vegetation or harvest group of cults, into more advanced and humanised concepts and religions, finally atrophying in the West with the collapse of Christianity as an institution. This does not, of course, close the story, for the racial responses and retentions of the theme have continued despite all collapses of known cults, and re-form or revert over and over again. The death-and-rebirth pattern is not merely limited to physical life-forms, but occurs in the realms of consciousness also. It is essential to consider the entire matter in terms of a flow of images, or of archetypes, rather than as a list of loosely related facts.

We can find remnants of the ancient cycle in several apocryphal folksongs connected with Jesus. For example, the *Cherry Tree Carol* presents quite clear images of a pagan type, including the ubiquitous Tree of Life (cf. section on *The Dilly Song* p. 73). Again, the carol *The Leaves of Life* (see song appendix) weaves a fascinating combination of pagan and apparently Christian symbols, again showing the Tree of Life, plus other tree and flower symbols of ancient magical meanihg.

The Bitter Withy, perhaps less obvious, expresses a myth in which only the Chosen One can cross the Bridge of Light and survive, let alone be able to return. The withy is the willow tree, sacred to the ancient Death Goddess. More obviously, we can turn to the famous *Lyke Wake Dirge* of the north of England for the proto-Christian and late pagan beliefs about the Other-world journey.

THE TWO MAGICIANS

*Oh she looked out of the window
as white as any milk—
and he looked in at the window as black as any
silk.*

CHORUS:
*Hullo hullo hullo hullo you coal-black smith,
and what is your silly song?
You never shall gain my maidenhead that I have
kept so long!
I'd rather I was dead, yes and then she said,
and be buried all in my grave,
than I'd have such a nasty husky dusky musty
fusty coal-black smith.
A maiden I will . . . die.*

*Then she became a hare, a hare all on the plain,
and he became a greyhound dog and chased her back again.*

*And she became a duck, a duck all on the stream,
and he became a water dog and fetched her back again.*

*Then she became a fly, a fly all in the air,
and he became a spider bold and dragged her to his lair.*

(other verses, ad. lib.)

This brief section of ballad is part of the best known magical song from
oral tradition. It was collected from a blacksmith of Minehead named

Sparks. Cecil Sharp notes, 'After collecting the song at Minehead, I questioned many Somerset singers about it, but except Mrs Welch of Ile Breuers, no one had any knowledge of it, and Mrs Welch could recall none of the tune, and only a line or so of the words.'

Despite a wide currency in Europe, and a long Scottish text, this magical-sequence song had almost passed out of the English tradition by the early twentieth century. The survival in the West Country, of a detailed magical ballad actually derived from a seasonal myth, even in shortened form, is nevertheless significant. The story itself is that of Little Gwion and Kerridwen, contained in the Myrvrian Archaeology of Wales. Originally a male child was pursued by the Goddess through the changing shapes or symbolic forms of the seasons and months. A similar echo of this theme is found in the Scots ballad, Tam Lin.

The origin of this shape-changing story is an ancient British religious Theme. (Out of all the magical songs within the oral tradition, it is *The Two Magicians* that has gained the greatest popularity as part of the current 'folk revival'.)

The melody from Mr Sparks the smith is probably a music-hall tune. Typically, the dominant sex has been reversed, and the man does the chasing and catching.

It would be interesting to see how this transposition copes with the rest of the ancient theme, in which the victim is reborn after the goddess has eaten him! On Sharp's admission, the words of the Somerset text were altered prior to publication as the term 'maidenhead' and the gaining thereof was not genteel enough for ladies and gentlemen who took a polite interest in quaint folksongs. The other known British text and the European variants make the matter quite clear—

> 'Well may you dress you lady fair
> Into your robes of red,
> Before the morn at this same time
> I'll gain your maidenhead.'
> TWO MAGICIANS, Child Vol. 1, No. 44

It has been suggested that shape-changing songs derive from tales of early saints, who were notorious for battling magically with evil pagan priests. This element of duel and transformation is well known in Christian hagiology, but the Gwion and Kerridwen tale pre-dates these mythically, and is poetically much closer to the folk ballads than any of the missionary contests. It is significant that there are no folksongs about saints contesting with pagans, whereas the pre-Christian modes of symbolism still survive in oral tradition. An examination of British folksong soon leads us to the conclusion that the British soul has remained essentially pagan, and true to a quite different life-spirit from that of our formalised worship.

The reversing of the sexual dominance brings us to the much discussed issue of matriarchy and patriarchy. The influence of this issue has obviously affected historical events, entire generations of attitude and servitude, and through religious and mythical influence governs the manner in which any society evolves. Should anyone be in doubt as to the value of studies of folklore and pagan myth, and their relevance to modern life, the answer is that these 'absurd tales' are the outer signs of the powers of human evolution that have put us in our present position. If we can begin to liberate ourselves, both collectively and individually, from the unconscious influence that is inherited from deliberate or accidental changes of these powers of consciousness, then we are moving towards a better world or future for us all. If we are restrained by ancient taboos through mere ignorance, or through religious or commercial conditioning, then we remain static, or even devolve for the profit of others who are able to manipulate such symbols.

Our racial mythology, and indeed that of all races, reveals that at one time the prevailing system of life was matriarchal—women were the ruling and dominant sex. At a later period the dominance was reversed, and men took the leading role. Today we may be swinging towards a period of joint equality, but sexual dominance is not a matter of muscles, penis or mammary glands, but of religion and magic.

The 'male era', which has given rise to various obsessions and preconceptions which enable men and women to be manipulated by other men and women, was the product of solar cult-worship, which gradually dominated the older lunar or other-world earth cults, in which the male hero was subservient to the Goddess.

The 'secret' of the solar cults, including Christianity, was that they held to inner or private forms of worship and ritual which depended upon the older system. We shall see, in the history of Saint George, that a male-orientated solar image was often used as the basis for a male human group or order—but that what they guarded was the sanctity of a feminine mystery. The Biblical expression of this is to be found in the early chapters of the book of Genesis, already showing signs of male-cult reinterpretation. The Tree of Life, of course, and the Garden, were magical and religious keys that were not limited to Semitic or Eastern origins.

It is interesting to remember that Joseph, the husband of the Virgin Mary, was not sanctified in the early Christian worship but seems to have been a minor figure who was later given emphasis. This implies the old matriarchal system, where the divinity (to say nothing of the

material inheritance) was through the female blood-line, not through
the male one.*

The validity of sexual supremacy is not in any way important to a
study of pagan lore, but religious and magical concepts and deep impulses that generate periods of sexual dominance obviously are of
primary importance. The entire worship pattern of *The Two Brothers*
may also be seen in this way, for one brother (Bran or the oracular
earth and death figure) was the hero-god of a matriarchal system, while
the other (Belin, the solar light and life figure) was the hero-god of a
male ascendancy. Even the wholly 'masculine' Saint George, however,
was linked to the cult of the Virgin Mary, as was his angelic archetype,
the Archangel Michael (see section on Saint George p. 61). We are
really examining in miniature a very complex cyclical issue, and there
is no historical or even cultural point of determination between absolute
'matriarchy' and absolute 'patriarchy'.

Folksongs seldom if ever have a 'God the Father' image within them,
and are often cited as being 'matriarchal'. Undoubtedly the mysterious
women who seem to regulate the ballad-world are ancient divine
images, for their actions identify them immediately, in their control
over birth and death, and in their magical powers. Even the magical
smith of *The Two Magicians* is merely usurping the hunting shapes of
the Goddess, not creating any new precedent of his own. The men of the
ballads are no primary 'God' images, but are an inseparable mixture
of lesser deities and their human hero-king-victims.

The root of the mystery, and of the Mysteries, derives from the
concepts of earth-as-mother, or earth-as-womb and tomb, and as
vessel and cauldron of life. When life was later identified with the
powers of the sun the masculine element gradually grew, but all aspects
of all gods and goddesses are both positive and negative, both good
and evil. Eventually the symbolism reduces to the absolutes of plus
and minus, without any definitive numbers.

The images found in our folk-material reflect the ancient systems, and
agree quite closely with those of classical and formal religious records.
It is usual to interpret folk-lore in the terms of classical mythology of
Greece and Rome, but a better and more productive method is to
follow the images themselves, and find where they lead us.

---

*See, for example, the genealogies offered by Luke, chapter one,
and by Matthew, chapter one. Whereas Matthew follows the male
line of inheritance, in the patriarchal fashion, Luke gives an entirely
different significance. He follows an older faith by stating that both
John the Baptist and Jesus Christ were miraculous births, brought
about by the mediation of the Archangel Gabriel.

The mothers of each of these men of God were related and 'of the
daughters of Aaron'.

There are two broad categories of pagan material in traditional song. The first is the obviously ritual material found in songs connected with folk-dramas and seasonal ceremonies, songs that portray a clear ritual action such as *The Cutty Wren* and the various May songs. Secondly, there are the many 'ancient' ballads, which use established mythological images either directly or indirectly in their plots. Additionally, there is subsidiary action and superstition which runs through a far wider body of songs, such as herb-lore, popular superstition regarding death and haunting, the influence of Other-worldly beings on humans, and general material related to luck, love, and death, which lives often un-noticed in traditional plots. This type of material is obviously mingled with the mythological themes of many ballads, but as time passes and the superstitious elements are forgotten or discredited they tend to drop out of use, while the basic images remain.

These basic images are timeless in that they exist out of historical time or context of religion and cult, and are 'true' in two ways. Firstly they represent ingredients of human consciousness related directly to men and women living with each other and with their fellow creatures in their native environment. Secondly, they act as cosmic symbols, or representations of apparent natural laws, which were eventually realised to exist through and beyond individual awareness and to be part of the basic pattern of existence. *The Two Brothers* is a manifestation of much more than a native cult originally dependent on an instinctive recognition of the need for gene mixture in human breeding.

The natural powers were associated with various images. The most primitive are probably those of beasts and birds—the Hare, the Bull, the Hawk, the Heron, the Crow, the Ram; they also include the Dove, the Fish, the Eagle, and the Lamb of Christian symbolism. The function and power of these creatures is transformed into a symbolic link with life-power itself, whether as nature, mankind or god. At a later stage, these key symbols become anthropomorphic, though not entirely. All deities have animal or bird forms or attributes, all have symbolic cult-beasts that are connected with them. Thus Bran and the Raven, Belinus and the Horse, Kerridwen and the Sow and so on through the entire company of divinities.

The fine points of definition in considering folksongs are not the timeless images themselves, of course, but their attributes shown through the superstitions found in their songs and tales. This working-rule for analysis does not affect the recognition of mythical material in the skeletal ballads, but it does prevent us from attempting accurate cult definition. No really convincing assessment of ancient British mythology exists, as the factual evidence is fragmentary, contradictory, tampered-with and confusing. Celtic deities, for example, merge into one another with the ease of the shape-changing of Kerridwen while we childishly demand that they stand still to be counted.

While retaining general concepts and images, it is more than likely that our ancient gods and goddesses in this sacred island changed their form throughout the year, and also over longer observed periods of solar and stellar passage. This would explain why the mythology seems so slippery when we attempt to force it into foreign moulds. The entire study of native mythology is still highly coloured by the carefully disguised readings of classical myths of Greece and Rome, when in fact a much broader view and base should be adopted.

Meanwhile, dreams and images and symbols are not logical, they are not regular, and they do not remain to be catalogued in detail. Why should a goddess be the same today as she was yesterday—and who are we to demand that she stays the same tomorrow? The nature of a dream or magical power is constant, but its *form* changes. Madness lies in fixity of thought and not in fluidity. The simplest way to examine the pagan material is to look at the characters of the folksongs and compare them with divine or heroic figures known to us from the old religions. Closer analysis may later reveal, as in the Padstow song, that actual details such as names and emblems will link apparently unconnected song-themes, and also reveal a surprisingly close derivation from pre-Christian faiths.

The Hero is the most immediately recognisable image in folksong. In addition to obviously dramatic activities such as rescuing maidens and slaying monsters, he is found in various disguises performing activities which he would not do were he a modern film or television character. The development of the modern 'anti-hero' is not necessarily related to the actions of the mythical hero. The contemporary fictional character who murders or rapes but is still a 'hero' is not a divine figure, but the product of commercialism designed to titillate through 'reality'. When tragic heroes perform acts in myth or folk-tale, they are moving along magical and inevitable lines, and it is misleading and dangerous to suggest that the modern 'real' hero or depraved anti-hero is a similar figure. Rather he is the product of mass wishful-thinking epitomised through clever psychology. This develops a 'feedback' pattern in which the character has gradually to become more and more depraved in order to stimulate the appetites of the consumer. This role is also fulfilled by other symbols such as great natural or unnatural disasters, monstrous beasts and thrilling diseases, generally reflecting the tensions of a vastly overcrowded planet.

The apparently guilty murderer of *The Two Brothers* is nevertheless the Hero, and his quality is not to be judged by superficial standards. The bloodthirsty villain of the gruesome ballad *Long Langkin* (see song appendix) is again the Hero, although he murders an innocent child and its mother for ill-defined reasons. The literal reading of ballad-plots often conceals an older and deeper flow of images which should be re-examined as a sequence of pictures, in much the same way as dream or visionary sequences appear to the inner eye. A reappraisal of the stories in this fashion will reveal quite distinct themes which are often identical with the key myths and divine personae of the pagan religions. In considering the images in this way, we are looking at the remains of ancient myths retained through oral tradition and also the regeneration of these same living patterns from the racial awareness. It is impossible to separate the first process from the second, as the intuitive appeal of basic patterns links them to human life and ritual expression, but such patterns also develop spontaneously from reaction to the environment itself.

Children will evolve ritual games from play and improvised action which link directly to ancient religious and magical forms. Obviously such games are not handed down, especially today, from an immemorial past but occur naturally within the group play.

The villain of *Long Langkin* may be a fairly close relative of Saint George. Many ballad stories as told and retained in the oral tradition are likely to be revisions of religious parables or myths. Such revisions are known to occur for two reasons. Initially a deliberate revision is always carried out with the advent of a new cult or aspect of faith, as when the Catholic Saints adopted the functions of the older gods and goddesses. A later stage in this process is the interpreting of ancient stories after their original meaning has been lost.

A further possibility is that the images themselves are exactly those which tend to occur in abnormal states of mind such as self-induced trances or drug-imposed visions. The oral tradition of magical ballads may well be one aspect of the pagan 'underground' survival, continued through the secret rites and folk-practices common to every part of Britain. The tradition of certain individuals learning their tunes and songs from the fairies (or later, the devil), suggests magical development or regeneration of songs and music in this fashion. If this visionary function and the magical utterance of 'jubilations' are linked, we have the oracular process of the pagan rites complete (see Chambers, FOLKSONG-PLAINSONG—also following section 'Musical considerations').

Formal religion of any sort is a means of relating and interpreting these deep images and urges in the most comprehensive manner possible for a large number of people. Today this function is carried out by television, and Saint George and his radiant line of spiritual predecessors are obliged to manifest themselves through the media characters. The grip of the expert manipulator upon the mass mind reaches its peak in television, which succeeds in obliterating or redirecting the urges which the Christian religion failed to cope with.

The Hero is the male figure in a specific ritualised behaviour-pattern within a song, tale or ballad. In the folksongs themselves he is generally a murderer, a victim, or a rescuer. Specific personalities of the hero, such as Robin Hood, merge into popular history and have a literary branch to their family tree. Nevertheless, Robin retains much of his mythical origin in his important roles in folk-drama and ritual. The names of the Hero are many, but his basic function is the same: championship and sacrifice.

The Heroine is a more complex character, if possible, than the Hero. She has various aspects—of mother, lover, and maiden. She appears as the villainous Mother who causes her son's or husband's death; and as the Mother who judges her son's action in several ritualised situations. She is also the lover who murders her man, as in *Lord Randall* or, more obscurely, in Giles Collins (see appendix). In this particular ballad she shows herself as maiden, lover, sister, mother, murderess and finally mourner. All that is needed is the magical revival, or natural rebirth of *The Two Brothers* theme to show her to be the ancient Triple Goddess, common to all religions. In some ballads she plays the part of victim, as in *Jackson and Johnson*, *Long Langkin* etc. This is rather a deceitful role in some cases, as she becomes an apparent victim only to murder the hero, after having taken her pleasure of him. In certain ballads one has the suspicion that the original point of the story has been lost or altered, as we know to be the case with Saint George, the maiden and the dragon (see p. 61ff). Occasionally she reveals her magical nature, as in the shape-changing of *The Two Magicians* or the witchcraft of *The Lailly Worm* and *Giles Collins*.

The villain is the twin of the Hero, and either one of them is liable to kill the other and be revived or reborn as we find in the songs and in plays alike. Ritual murder is a very common theme of magical ballads, with or without revival. There is a quite noticeable difference between a ritual ballad and any other folk or popular song which involves murder. Many of the eighteenth- or nineteenth-century broadside plots involve murder, usually of innocent but pregnant maidens. Often these songs utilise popular superstition, such as the ghost of the wronged innocent appearing and denouncing, or even killing, the murderer. Such cases however, do not have the ritual element or style, as they are essentially blood-and-melodrama pieces, written for popular appeal. They stand in the same relationship to the ritual ballads as the popular Sunday newspapers and thrillers do to great tragic plays and novels. The entire unfolding of a magical ballad is impersonal and inevitable, with no moral, and often, no conclusion.

The undeniable ritual element is that of the magical ceremony where certain acts and words, analogous to spiritual processes, must be carried out in certain specific rhythms and order. Only when the act is done in the manner prescribed can results be obtained. This same analogous form of thought is obvious in the seasonal ritual folk-plays where the victim is formally killed and then revived. Such an act is the human contribution to the flow of the seasons and surrounding life of all kinds.

Brother murders brother for possession of true love! If this were a newspaper headline, we should certainly expect no nonsense about ritual or pagan faiths. When this murder occurs in a ballad or folk-play we find that no-one is shocked by the actual murder: it is calmly accepted, but the significance lies in what happens after the act. The key part of the tale is in the revival, or in the ritual questions, and no-one seems to ascribe guilt for the murder or demand retribution, as one would expect. Some versions of the tale turn the brothers into acceptable characters such as Saint George and the Turkish Knight, but these are obviously later rationalisations.

The ritualised murder may sometimes be found in ballad-plots without the 'two brothers' motif, mainly instances where the woman murders the man for an unknown reason. The general character of a ritual plot seems to be its apparent pointlessness, or the total lack of any information on the cause of the tragedy involved.

BRUTON TOWN

In Bruton town there lived a farmer
he had three sons and a daughter dear,
by day and night they were contriving
to fill their parents' hearts with fear.

One told his secret to none other
but unto his brother this he said,
I think our servant courts our sister,
I think that they have a mind to wed.

If he our servant courts our sister
that maid from such a shame I'll save
I'll put an end to all his courtship
and send him silent to his grave.

A day of hunting was prepared
in thorny brakes where the briars grew,
and there they did this young man murder
and into the brake his fair body threw.

Oh welcome home my darling brothers,
our servant dear is he behind?
We've left him where we've been out hunting,
we've left him where no man can find.

She went to bed crying and lamenting,
lamenting for her own true love.
She slept and dreamed that she saw him by her
all covered o'er in a gore of blood.

Do you wake up early tomorrow morning
and unto the garden brake d'you go,
and there you'll find my body lying,
'twas your own three brothers that laid me low.

She woke up early the very next morning
and to the garden brake she did go.
'Twas there she found her own dear jewel
in the same place where the briars do grow.

Now since my brothers have been so cruel
as to take your tender sweet life away,
one grave shall hold us both together
and along with you in death I'll stay.

This song—collected in Somerset by Cecil Sharp—is one of the rare examples of folk-lore and literary tradition exchanging material, and finally returning to an oral currency. The song itself contains certain magical themes, but is not typical of a ritual ballad. It has neither the style nor the starkness of plot of other ritual songs, being a typical hack re-written piece. The variants collected in the United States as well as in the West Country are preserved through the medium of the broadsheet, and still bear the distinctive marks of cheap song style.

There is also a well established literary tradition for the story, from Boccaccio through to Keats' mawkish pseudo-ballad. The origin of the tale in the *Decameron* is undoubtedly traditional and has all the content of a ritual murder. A group of young men collectively murder a victim for the sake of a woman. She then digs up his body, and severs the head. This is kept, and planted with the herb basil, the discovery of the murder having been initiated by the ghost of the dead victim in a dream. The images here seem to be sacrificial, with a group of men bearing collective responsibility for the murder, a concept well known from classical sources and from surviving European folk-plays and dance-dramas.

The ritual use of the severed head was an important aspect of Celtic religion, deriving from the primitive cults of the dead and from ancestor-worship. This practice is oracular, as was the famous head of Bran, the spirit of the victim being linked to his severed head for a certain period of time. The theme of the magical head continued through into the medieval period with the brazen heads of the master magicians such as Albertus Magnus. The concept, however, is not present in the variants of *Bruton Town* collected from the folk sources, although the writer of the (presumably) nineteenth-century broadsheet would have been familar with it, from Boccaccio.

The song collected from the Somerset singer is quite literary in style, and poses some interesting questions. A long version of the story is inscribed on the wall of a public-house in Bruton—but did the broadsheet-writer derive his material from literary sources or from an existing folksong? Where and when was the melody now sung linked to the text? . . . It is more accurate to trace genuine folksong from an oral tradition than to attempt to trace pieces that have attained printed currency. The folksong is an organic and unconscious development that persists independently of written material; the commercial song-sheet is not part of a non-literate culture, nor does it retain its myths through story and song handed down over the generations.

Bruton Town has all the marks of folk superstition. The dream revelation of the murder is a typical theme, as the dying of grief. Whoever put his version of the ancient story together knew his market. The filling-in of actual details, such as the name of any town or the occupation of the father, a general background for the drama, is not at all typical of the mythological or otherwise ancient songs, which dive straight to the heart of the matter with no preamble, and are timeless.

Bruton Town thus bridges the distance between folk-lore and folk-song proper, and that which has been absorbed by a literary and commercial tradition. There is very little material that, having crossed the border into 'respectability', actually reverts to oral status at a later date. The song itself has a powerful and dramatic melody which more than compensates for the lengthy exposition of the plot; it must be remembered that the music of traditional songs in Britain was always subsidiary to the plot (see 'Musical Considerations' p. 95).

The same ritual group-murder is found in the song—

THE THREE BUTCHERS

(Text: Frank Stockley, Wareham, Dorset; air: William Cousins, Bath)

It's of three jolly butchers as I have heard men say
They were going to some market town their money for to pay.

They rode together for a mile or two and a little more beside,
Said Johnson unto Jipson, I heard a woman cry.

Then 'Stop I Won't' said Jipson, and 'Stop I won't' said Ryde,
Then 'Stop I will' said Johnson, 'for I heard a woman cry.'

So Johnson he alighted and viewed the place all round
And he saw a naked woman with her hair pinned to the ground.

How come you here, said Johnson, how came you here said he?
The highwaymen have robbed me, as you can plainly see.

Then Johnson being a valiant man and a man of courage bold,
He took the coat from off his back to keep her from the cold.

And Johnson being a valiant man, of valiant mind,
He sat her up upon his horse and mounted up behind.

And as they rode along the road as fast as they could ride,
She put her fingers to her lips and gave three piercing cries.

Out sprang ten bold highwaymen with weapons in their hands,
They stepped up to young Johnson and boldly bid him stand.

'Then stand I will' said Johnson, 'as long as ever I can,
For I never was in all my life afraid of any man.'

And Johnson being a valiant man he made those bullets fly,
Till nine of them ten highwaymen all on the ground did lie.

Now this wicked woman standing by young Johnson did not mind,
She took a knife all from his side and stabbed him from behind.

But the day it being market day and people passing by,
They saw this woman's dreadful deed and raised a hue and cry.

Then she was down to Newgate brought, bound down in irons strong,
For killing the finest butcher as ever the sun shone on.

This very widespread ballad was collected in Bath. All known texts generally tell the same story, which appeared in broadsheet form in the nineteenth century.

At first glance there might appear to be no magical-religious material in this song, but it is quite possible that it is derived from an early theme, as it has the recognisable elements common to mythical stories. The nineteenth-century dressing does not disguise the development of the action, which is ritualistic in the same fashion as *The Two Brothers*, *Edward*, *Long Langkin* or any other ancient ballad.

The story is simply as follows: A man finds a woman pinned by her hair—he cuts her free, but is attacked by a group of men, his assistant(s) running away. He fights the attackers and conquers them, but is stabbed in the back by the woman, and dies. In the elaborated version the woman is caught, but usually the ballad ends with the hero's death.

The images of the ballad suggest that it was based upon an older song or visual theme dealing with the sacrificial rite common to most folk-memories of pagan worship—linking an Egyptian myth with the story of OSIRIS and his collective murder.*

Possibly the evil heroine here is not simply killing the victim, but cutting out his magical heart or name as ISIS does, in the Egyptian variant.

The woman tied by her hair is typical of the hero myth, as for example that of Saint George or Perseus, and in earlier legends. The logical explanation, that in this song she was a robber's accomplice, is typical literary aetiology. But the entire development of the plot has a curious inevitability that is the hallmark of a much older ballad. Why did the woman not assist her fellow robbers in the beginning of the battle—why wait until all were dead before killing the hero?—clearly a common-sense explanation of the plot does not hold together. The group-attack is reminiscent of the classically recorded collective responsibility for the ritual murder, suggested also perhaps in *Bruton*

---

*And Celtic stories of ritual king-murder, particularly in the folk tradition.

Town. There is a great temptation to accept, with songs of this sort, Graves's theory that many myths are derived from a misreading of religious pictures or icons. It is not necessary, however, for such images to have actually existed as material pictures, for they are self-perpetuating symbolic sequences within the group-mind of the people or peoples who maintain such themes within their tradition.

Possible sources of this story are numerous, but what has to be considered is the general nature of the imagery, as it is impossible to pin down the sources of origin of material of this type. The farther the 'original' is pursued, the more elusive it becomes and the more heads it seems to grow.

Songs not Magical

It is easy to over-emphasise the magical or mythical content of particular folksongs, and difficult indeed to attempt to define the point at which ordinary songs become magical, or pagan lore becomes everyday superstition. Songs such as *Bruton Town* and *The Three Butchers* pose real problems of definition, but also give insight into the complex routes that ancient images can travel.

The actual proportion of songs that may be defined as 'pagan' in some way or other is very small indeed, if we examine obvious statistics. The method suggested in this book—that we adopt an interpretation of images within a certain group of stylised folksongs—increases the number of magical or religious songs considerably. It would be pointless to apply a broader analysis of imagery to any and every folksong, as most songs are exactly what they appear on the surface. There is an area in which early religious imagery and basic psychic ingredients overlap, which is only to be expected as primitive faith or worship is never intellectually divorced from human experience. It is arguable that certain songs are ritualistic merely by unconscious coincidence, but this ignores the fact that ritual evolves spontaneously from human society, and is not formalised until it begins to accumulate a body of beliefs common to a larger number of individuals. At this stage it becomes necessary to preserve ritual patterns from decay through an intellectual system, and this is exactly the point at which all mass religions have begun to decay. The ritual images in folksong are devoid of cult or rule because they are the basic elements, the foundation-blocks of religion, and as such cannot be coincidental with pagan myth, as they are the origins of *all* myths. When examining folksongs we are looking not only at the remains of early beliefs, but at the roots of those same beliefs stripped of most of their superficial growth through common use. These roots are continually regenerated in the same way and through the same power as the divine hero-victim whose story they tell.

In actual study or analysis symbolic methods should never be applied indiscriminately, but must be reinforced by a considerable knowledge of style, historical context, and general identification of classes of folksong. There are general rules, but as always with folksong, these rules are always being broken. The bulk of broadsheet popular material is not likely to hold ancient religious motifs, yet it is from this pseudo-literary source that the plot of *Bruton Town* passed back into the oral tradition. One would hardly imagine that music-hall pieces would contain any Celtic lore, yet to all appearances *The Two Magicians* is both a music-hall entertainment and clearly a version of the Welsh myth of Kerridwen. It is dangerous, then, to set any general rules or areas of research, other than obvious preferences for the sake of time and method. Many areas may be excluded, but can be returned to after more obvious sources have been studied. Drinking-songs, for example, are generally semi-literary and contain little or no folk-lore. *John Barleycorn* (typical of fertility myths such as those of Tammuz and other nature gods), collected in the West Country and elsewhere, is a magical song beyond doubt . . . and also a drinking song.

The common folk who sing them did not distinguish between magical ballads and sentimental popular songs, they merely sung whatever appealed to them. Ordinary statistical evidence shows that religious or magical songs and themes are a fairly low percentage of total collected material; but initial use of statistics in this manner is meaningless, because the areas of definition overlap and interweave, and are only susceptible to the broadest forms of proportional examination. There is a central body of ballads and songs, usually defined by style as well as content, that is clearly pagan and embodies the basic elements of the sacrificial ancient religions. In addition to this, the concepts themselves sometimes spring up in surprising forms and unexpected places—statistically most folksongs are not 'magical', but any of them may hold magical elements.

There are a large number of songs that contain popular superstition, but which are not strictly religious or mythical. Many obviously composed broadsheets reveal certain popular beliefs which are not direct evidence of pagan lore, although their retention in the folk-memory can often be traced to religious sources. Typical of such ideas is the constantly recurring murder-and-guilt concept, in which a murder is revealed by supernatural means. In later literary versions this is usually accomplished by the appearance of the victim's ghost, and the subsequent accusation or revenge belong in the realms of the horror story. These elements, however, are the degenerate remains of early magical concepts. For example, the victim's soul appearing as a bird still occurred in nineteenth-century broadsheets in the form it is found in several undatable magical ballads.

The writers of popular songs, therefore, catering for a mass market, were also preserving material from folk-sources, even when it was retrieved from an earlier literary use. Broadsheet songs form a very high proportion of the collected material, though many of them are not sensational but lyrical or simply romantic.

The great problem with any examination of collected traditional material is that it is frozen. As our own oral tradition is virtually extinct—and has been so for some years—we have an incredibly distorted picture to study. The main body of songs from the people are no earlier than the nineteenth century, though some are traceable to the previous century either directly or through oral metamorphosis. Yet there are songs and ballads undoubtedly older, some of which may be traced, but many of which seem to be perplexingly ancient and utterly untraceable. The implications behind this division of material is that the popular songs are taken up and forgotten within 50–100 years while the more primitive and basically magical songs are never totally lost. Commonplace songs vary with social conditions, with political expediency, with any and all of the changes that occur in any period of history. The magical songs, religious or mythical themes, are slow-changing and survive immense social disruption, to be retained within the folk-consciousness.

We know from literary sources that some of these ballads were being sung in previous centuries, yet the popular songs of these times have all but disappeared. The evidence suggests that the mythical and magical songs are the core of our traditional song repertoire around which all other material revolves. This is merely to say that there are certain vital images that remain constant, while others less deeply rooted rise and fall according to the tides of social development.

An analysis of this sort could, however, be misleading, as it deals exclusively with the evidence for magical and religious survivals in folksong. Folk-singers never sang 'magical' songs, but merely 'songs'. The situation is also coloured by the taste of the folksong collectors, especially the pioneers of the modern field. A great deal has been written about the prudery shown by Baring-Gould, Cecil Sharp and others, not only in their published works, but occasionally in manu-script as well. Added to this is the personal discretion of the folk singers themselves, who would not sing certain songs to the 'gentlemen', and certainly not ladies such as Lucy Broadwood, nor to men of the cloth. We may have lost several bawdy songs in this way, and quite a few music-hall pieces, much to be regretted if the censored or omitted songs were wedded to good traditional airs.

There are some examples of traditional informants who were quite unwilling to give details of their rituals, jealously guarded by close conservative attitudes. More than this, there are also those who still retained a conscious appreciation of their rites, and of the lore, such as Mr Crockford of Bratton, Minehead. His extremely evasive answers to Cecil Sharp (FSFS ser. V) when asked about the local wassail apple-orchard customs were quite clearly intended to give away no informa-tion. Crockford was one of a number of people, commented upon by collectors, who were locally acknowledged guardians of local custom and song. It is possible that these important village characters were the survivors of the old system of priestly inheritance (discussed later in 'The Survival of Pagan Cults' p. 107).

In the same region (Langport in Somerset), the vicar told Sharp that it was expressly forbidden to use wooden vessels for Holy Communion.

This survival from early interdicts against rival religions in which trees were closely identified with specific deities, was discussed at a time when the parishioners were still invoking fertility powers for their trees, and singing of the cup 'made of the good ashen tree' in their ritual wassail song.

More insidious than this, however, are the pre-conceptions from which our English folksong collectors tended to suffer. Baring-Gould, for example, was an extremely learned student of folk- and occult lore, and must certainly have been aware of the pagan element in the songs that he heard from time to time. His suppression of the mythical origin of Saint George in his *Lives of the Saints* shows clearly that he not only understood the pagan element in native British lore, but that he chose to ignore it when he felt this to be necessary for the furtherance of his beliefs. Their educated background caused collectors to alter lines and words in songs, unless they were utterly true to the material as heard. It is interesting to consider whether or not some of our collected folksongs have had their pagan clues removed, either by ignorance or through deliberate editing. When early collectors emphasised the freshness and purity of folksong and lyric they forgot that innocence is the prime quality of fertility-worship and pagan religion, and that one cannot collect the products of the race-mind and soul without also collecting the people's true religion.

A natural attitude to sexual matters so clearly stated in folksong was not at all approved by early collectors, who were looking mainly for material that could be patronised.

The general conditioning of the early part of this century in educated persons was Christian-male-cult by nature, and a true understanding of the essentially religious nature of many folksongs and activities was rare. Even those who noted such material still regarded it as quaint, or an interesting proof of the tenacity of the oral tradition, rather than as a living expression of unconscious worship.

Little wonder that rural celebrants were unwilling, possibly unable, to cross the abyss of non-communication between themselves and those cultured and intellectual collectors.

Despite the problems outlined it was difficult for song-collectors to avoid pagan material, especially when it was relatively anonymous, as in the songs examined here and in their many related variants. Even obviously pagan customs, however, have been misunderstood and once an opinion has been fixed in print it is difficult to convince researchers that they have to do anything more than copy it over and over again.

Despite the repeated appearance of 'Saint George' in tradition, the general attitude to this image is still that he is an interloper, something of

a nuisance in the folk-lore field who has obscured the issue and origin of
the folk-plays. In the following chapter we shall see that this is not so,
and perhaps help to restore Saint George to his rightful place as a
national symbol . . ..

Who is Saint George?

Saint George has been the cause of more speculative writing than most national saints, and poses a delicate problem for hagiologists. As we have seen, even the Rev. Sabine Baring-Gould, dedicated folksong collector and ardent student of the occult, went to great lengths to prove that the saint had an historical origin. Possibly the Anglican patriot vicar wanted to exorcise the unconsciously damning words of Pope Gelasius, who stated as early as A.D. 494 that George was 'one of those saints whose names were justly revered by men, but whose actions are known only to God'. Ex cathedra statements and learned discussions of Saint George are full of such casuistry.

In Butler's *Lives of the Saints*, however, the author admits that 'it is not quite clear how George came to be chosen to be Patron Saint of England'. Even relatively simple facts such as the dates for his official institution are confused.

'In 1222 the National Synod of Oxford instituted St George's day as a national holiday.'

'In 1220 St George became Patron Saint of England, and in 1222 his day was ordered to be observed as a national festival.'

'In 1395 St George became patron Saint of England.'

'In 1415 the constitution of Archbishop Chichele made St George's day one of the chief feasts of the year.'

One date is absolutely clear: in 1969 the Roman Catholic Church relegated St George to the status of local saint only—thus apparently concluding a long and glorious career.

The English national saint appears in various folk-rituals collected from tradition, and has a significant position in the Padstow May song. It has generally been assumed that he is a late intruder into these venerable happenings, but this is not the case. The historical mystery surrounding George's origins is not to be explained by his Christian career, nor is his appearance in native ritual due to his Crusading popularity. The secret of Saint George is that he is a pagan divine image. In discussion of this origin we will examine the Padstow May Song, and also look briefly into the origin of the Order of the Garter. These two apparently unrelated events and gatherings, which could hardly be further apart in circumstances, are spiritually both heirs of one and the same worship-pattern. They form important links in the evidence for a perpetuating pagan worship, and clarify the popularity of a particular image, that of the divine hero.

Even the briefest study of the material connected with his history shows that George has been disguised, but there are several holes in his Christian armour through which he may be clearly seen in his true aspect. The mystery commented upon by Butler, and perpetuated by Baring-Gould, was contrived because George was no stranger to

Britain, and his appearance as an Eastern saint was actually a re-introduction or absorption process whereby he replaced a pagan god still venerated by the common people. The attributes and origins of the two beings were identical in many respects, but like most absorption processes, there was a later attempt at concealment by a more strongly established authority. George was turned into a respectable citizen, sometimes identified with a Cappadocian pork-butcher of the fourth century, in an attempt to give him historical credibility. This absorption is typified by the famous quotation from Gregory the Great, found in Bede's *History*. The phrasing is curiously echoed by a later, much later, attempt to replace the Padstow Ceremony with an ox-roast, in the nineteenth century.

Do not after all pull down the fanes. Destroy the idols, purify the buildings with holy water, set relics there and let them become temples of the true God. So the people will have no need to change their places of concourse, and where of old they were wont to sacrifice cattle to demons, thither let them come on the day of the saint to whom the church is dedicated, and slay the beasts no longer as a sacrifice but for a social meal in honour of Him whom they now worship.

The confused accounts of George's martyrdom are aspects of a general theme, by no means exclusively Christian. The story has it that he was tortured for his faith but was miraculously revived several times before dying. His eventual death assured him of a place in heaven and his body and head became objects of veneration and sources of miracles. His cult gradually spread outwards and westwards from its centre at Lydda until he was taken up in England. His story is very close to that of any number of sacrifical myths, so should not be accepted at face value. Prior to George, Edward the Confessor was patron-saint of England, yet no popular memory of him remains. Why should a relatively recent saint be the object of such adulation, and remain alive within the folk images? His identity rests within his symbolic attributes, for after his formal torture and ritual death he is translated to heaven, where his great purity and virtue make him a guardian of goodness and a defender against evil. The slaying of the Dragon was never an historical event, but is a mythical theme known all over the ancient world. The monster symbolises evil power or rather, primordial chaos, which is controlled by an intelligence of Light. This entire theme was merely Christianised to provide an officially acceptable focus for energies and worship already given to such images by the native peoples. The earthly Saint George is remarkably similar to the heavenly Archangel Michael, who is also shown as controlling or slaying a serpent or dragon, but is acknowledged as a metaphysical power, and never forced into material reality.

The British Saint George is a divine hero; he combines several aspects of Heroism, and represents the roots of various cultures, myths and gods. His invincibility in arms, his heroic rescue of a princess, and his dragon-killing are the formal functions he carries out. In folk-drama and legend he also fights and slays the Turkish Knight—a typical adaptation of the dark-and-light-brother theme—and is found in the place of the sacred king or hero who travels to the Other-world. That journey is suggested in the dirge of the Padstow May Song, which has links with the last verse of *The Two Brothers* or *Edward*, already described:

> 'Oh where is Saint George, where is he Oh?
> He's out in his longboat,
> All on the salt sea oh!'

The Two Brothers, or personified powers of light and dark or summer and winter, do battle. The loser is brought back to life by the Goddess, and in turn conquers, but in sophisticated versions of the myth he does not slay his rival, but subdues him. Presumably the reasoning behind this is that a controlled chaotic power will not arise again afresh, and we find that Archangel Michael does not destroy the Serpent, but controls Him, pending rehabilitation in the divine scheme of perfection.*

The miraculous powers ascribed to Saint George are simply those of the Divine King or Hero who crosses the Abyss after ritual death, and is expected to guide his people from the Other-world. The particular emphasis given to George during the Crusades shows him to be a lively re-generation of a national power-figure, a solar and victorious being. It is difficult to disentangle the personality or manifestation of any deity, as Hero or Sacrificial Victim, from the abstract image of the god itself. The two, one eternal and unchanging, the other subject to personal and cultural fluctuation, are easily confused, not only through historical and mythical distortion in time but also in the minds of the original worshippers themselves. The most complex arguments of this problem are probably those relating to the question of Christ's humanity or Divinity, which were not resolved until quite a late period, and then only by decree. One good reason for making Saint George an actual human being was to claim that he received a manifestation of Christian divine power, rather than that he re-formed himself under another name to suit the times.

The development of George as an Eastern saint is worth considering and comparing with his Western prototype. The popular figure whose

---

*This phase also marks a change in ritual custom

cult spread to Britain was an offshoot of another saint altogether, who has almost disappeared from view. Pre-dating George, with exactly the same theme and attributes, was the immensely popular Eastern figure, St Mena. The histories of both in early lives of the saints are identical on details such as their military career and their persecution by a tyrannical Emperor. By the fourth century A.D. there was a basilica to St Mena near Alexandria. During the present century this church, which had been lost for a long period of time, was rediscovered, excavated and researched by a team of archaeologists. The surface Christian buildings were found to have been built over an ancient pagan temple-cave containing Egyptian figures and images. The basic image of the man killing the dragon may be traced to that of Horus, the Egyptian Divine Child Harpocrates triumphing over Set. St Mena had absorbed a cult deriving from ancient Egypt, then was in turn absorbed by Saint George, possibly in an attempt to draw Eastern Christian energy away from the obviously pagan faith.

The saving of the Princess from the Dragon, closely connected to the Greek myth of Perseus, was partly a rationalisation or conversion of the original myth in which the brothers battle before various aspects of the Goddess herself.

Saint George of the mummers' plays, although taking his name and popularity from an eastern source, is an extension of a native hero or god. At one period he seemed set as the English substitute for Archangel Michael, and the defiant Henry the Eighth placed his image upon coins where that of Michael had previously appeared. This act may have been prompted by the defection from Papal authority, and the development of Saint George within the Order of The Garter suggests that he was intended to be a uniquely English divine mediator.

George is intimately connected in folk-custom with the May ceremonies, those fertility rites of unknown origin. The first of May, traditionally the first day of summer as the Padstow song tells us, dates back to the feast of Beltane. This was one of the great festivals of the native religion which passed into folk-practice and was never successfully banned by Christian authority, although the usual absorption attempts were made. Several significant dates occur in early May, bearing in mind calendar changes. May the eighth is St Michael's day. This Archangel is said to be the keeper of the keys to the Bottomless Pit or Abyss, where the demonic powers are confirmed. His placement close upon the day of Bel, a Celtic Solar Deity, is no accident. The word Beltane translates roughly as 'brilliant star'—exactly the attribute of Archangel Michael. We thus have the amusing picture of the Christian power-symbol keeping down himself in an earlier shape, now considered to be an evil pagan demon. As the Devil himself, as Lucifer, was once a great angelic power, this absurdity should not be too much of a surprise. The pagan hilltop-sites were rededicated to Michael, to guard against pagan infiltration, yet he was nothing more than an adopted Semitic image for a figure already worshipped in the West.

Old Saint George's day was 4 May (now 23 April due to the introduction of Gregory's Calender in 1752)—4 May was the final day of the May ceremonies, and George was considered to be an incarnation of the powers represented by Michael in heroic form. George is usually shown to be a mounted figure, and it is worth noting that the Celtic diety Beli(nus) was connected with a horse or horses as part of his solar symbolism. Belinus may be traced to the root word BEL, best known as the Babylonian deity who slew the sea-beast Tiamat (George and the Dragon). There is a fine mythological line to be traced here, leading Michael to his hilltop and hell-keeping role. According to Graves (*The White Goddess*) the name Bel or Belili was the origin of the Biblical expression 'sons of Belyial'. In the Semitic tongue this word meant 'Hell', or a place from which one did not arise again, though it was not originally a Semitic term at all. St Michael, annexing the feast of Beltane from his predecessor, reaches further in time and distance than we might expect. There is no real need, however, for this clever linguistic explanation. The replacing of one culture's god or image by that of another is well known, and works all the better if they are simply aspects of one proto-typical divine power. As Bel fought and conquered Tiamat, so did Saint George fight and conquer the Dragon. As Beli slew his brother Bran, in the cultural and seasonal myth, so does Saint George in mummer's plays slay the Turkish Knight. This transfers the cultural battle from one era to another, but does not alter the metaphysical symbolism, the root appeal which keeps the myth alive.

In the Padstow May song, George is not being martyred directly, though he is mentioned in the dirge when the 'Obby Oss' dies, nor is he slaying Dragons.

Instead, he goes out to sea in a longboat. This identifies him with the brother in the bottomless boat (*Edward*), and with numerous mythological characters who do exactly the same thing. That this journey occurs during the death of the 'Oss is interesting, as the melody for the dirge sung at this point in the ritual is identical to that of the wren ritual-song from distant Pembrokeshire. The Wren, curiously enough, was the symbol of Beli's 'brother', Bran.*

---

*This is one of several interesting examples of the inter-relationship of lore, ritual and music that occur around the west coasts of Britain and the shores of Ireland. The inference is that contact by sea spread certain ritual patterns to coastal ports, patterns which are connected in inland communities.

The lines of part of the Padstow song suggest that there may at one time have been a ritual ship in the procession.

> 'The young men of Padstow they might if they would,
> They might have built a ship and gilded her with gold'.

The May-ship is a processional device found all over Europe, and was not only connected with shipbuilding communities. It was actually a symbolic vessel such as the various arks, trees, ships and cradles in which Divine Children and mother goddesses were found, cast afloat upon the Ocean of Eternity, the Mother Deep. As late as the twelfth century a monk of St Trond described (in 1133) the building of a pagan ship and the orgiastic worship attending it. In this case the passenger was not the divine son, but the Mother herself, as an image of the fertile earth. Even the most sophisticated type of mystical thinking has used the analogy of a vessel upon the sea of all time or space, in which the Saviour, of any name, travels.

If we trace Saint George to St Michael to Beli, we come to *The Two Brothers*, the root image. This in turn leads us to the Egyptian myth which later evolved the cult of St Mena, who was superseded by Saint George. If we travel in the bottomless boat with the brother of the folksong, we see his other identity as Hercules, and finally as another Celtic God, OGMIAS. This deity 'of sun-like countenance' was a champion divine, classically identified with Hercules because of his functions and attributes. Ogmias invented the ancient alphabet of Ogham, and is one-who-binds, either through the magic of his words, or through the phallic power of his club or staff. This staff later became the long spear or lance of justice of St Michael, and was also found as the judgement-stick of Anubis in Egyptian myth. An ancient image of Ogmias shows him leading a troop of men by chains attached to his tongue.

A further conceptual link, discussed more closely in the section on musical considerations, is that the Ogham* alphabet is closely connected with the chant-systems of the Druid or native religion. Ecclesiastical plainsong in the West is likely to have derived from this source, and is aimed specifically at making 'other-world' contact. Ogmias is therefore the presiding deity of magical music, so it should be no great surprise to find that Archangel Michael is regent of the Sphere of Harmony in Hebrew mysticism. Ogmias acts as psychopomp leading souls to the Other-world—as does Michael—weighing them in the balance with his staff and interceding for them 'before the Highest throne'. As magical chanting was originally a means of linking, through trance, the seeress or medium with the spirit of the sacrificial victim,

---

*An early Celtic alphabet code, with various forms.

we can trace a line or evolution from primitive to sophisticated religious practice.

The deity most famed for music was Apollo. He also was linked with the horse, as was Belinus or Bel, and the priests of Apollo practised healing and oracular trance through the use of music. The strings of his lyre had a particular mystical significance, probably that of the seven planets, one for each string. The basic notes of plainsong-modes are seven, with no chromatic intervals allowed. The Archangel Michael was invoked for healing energies, as he mediated the harmonising and health-bestowing energies of the Sun—the planet of Apollo. Little wonder that Saint George's tomb had miraculous healing powers.

As a fertility-power, George is known as Jack-in-the-Green, or the Green-man, or Green George. He returns to leaf and life after the triumph of winter, and the attempt to merge him with the Eastern Christian Saint George has merely helped to perpetuate his rites.

There was no hard dividing-line between orthodox and pagan worship in England at the time of George's rise to prominence. Vested authority was officially Christian, but many groups and individual priests are known to have carried out pagan forms of worship, while the bulk of the population was pagan, as it had always been. Apart from this ecclesiastical paganism, the structure of royalty, nobility or chivalry was based upon ancient and deep religious foundations, generally *pre*-Roman. The appearance of Saint George as patron of the Order of the Garter was originally nothing to do with the modern concept of polite chivalrous behaviour, but stems from the Order's revival as a religious body linked to the concept of Divine Kingship.

The arguable 'Divine Right of Kings' which caused so much trouble in Britain has a much older origin and deeper roots than is at first realised. The divine right stems from the pre-Christian religion, when the king's right to rule was balanced by the people's right to sacrifice him. Perhaps poor King Charles Stuart was only fulfilling an inherited fate; certainly the common folk lost no time in identifying him with numerous large oak-trees throughout the country. The oak was the sacrificial tree of the Sacred King and, of course, the tree of the god Bel.

The Order of the Garter was a re-working of a 'holy blood' system, by which a continual line of inheritance was sought through careful breeding. The origin of this was an attempt to incarnate special souls, though it later degenerated into the exclusive club of the inbred aristocracy.

The 'scandalous' activities of nuns, monks and priests, who were rumoured to have sexual relationships in secret, is more than a mere dirty story or political propaganda. It is an aspect of folk-memory, reinforced by the fact that convents were often built on ancient sacred sites, and linked by tunnels originally used in the anonymous breeding-rituals common in the ancient world.

The image of George, and his connection with an exclusive royal blood order, struck a responsive chord in this racial memory. The Order was supposed to have been prompted by the famous Garter incident, learned at one time by every schoolboy and never explained in a satisfactory manner.

The Beltane festival has links with the ancient Latin festival of Parilia (though this does not suggest that it is derived from it—they were merely aspects of a common rite.) Fraser suggests (in *The Golden Bough*) that this was a love festival, a holy breeding-ceremony exempt from normal moral rules. Violet Alford observed the same break from strict Catholic morality in the celebrants of the Bear rituals of French Catalonia. The Padstow May Ceremony is also rough and fertile, working up to a frenzy even today that is reminiscent of an older world altogether than that of the seething tourists who block the way of the ritual dancers.

The garbled tale about the Duchess of Salisbury and her 'garter' may refer to her royalty of blood, according to the matriarchal system, where inheritance of any sort was through the female line. The pagan festivals such as Parilia or May-rites were not simply licentious orgies, but attempts at a breeding pattern which was a special part of the religion itself. The white and red roses of the Order of the Garter are typical 'blood' symbols; they appear in the Padstow song, and also in *Down in Yon Forest* and various other ritual songs.

Saint George was the divine Hero image derived from Belinus, the later Celtic solar deity who superseded Bran, an early and chthonic god. He guarded and inspired members of a chosen order of sacred kings or sacrificial victims, whose blood-line was probably inherited from the female side. The much-pursued Duchess of Salisbury must have held this ancient blood line, as maintained by the matriarchal system, for no other reason can explain her career. The attributes of the god image or 'Saint' were supposed to be the aspiration of the male members of the Order, and this Being would be expected to be their guide and helper in both outer and inner worlds. Saint George was supposed to have led the knights in victorious battle against the heathen, but in vision not in flesh. That such an Order was established, or according to some authorities re-established, by an apparently Christian monarchy is interesting, but more amazing altogether is George's folk popularity, and the overall fact that both extremes of the population worshipped and portrayed the same figure.

There is also supposed to be a general connection between the Order of the Garter and the Order of the Holy Grail, and it was intended in part to be a re-established version of the Round Table of King Arthur.

The entire concept was dedicated to the Virgin Mary, under the guardianship of SS George and Michael, and such a typical hierarchical pattern is merely that of the Ancient Mysteries. Under overall power of the Goddess, the Divine Son in Heaven operates through his lesser divinities or regents, and through his earthly incarnation, either in the flesh, or deceased, but still active in the spirit world. An astonishingly oblique analysis of the subject can be found in the work of the nineteenth-century writer Hargrave Jennings (*The Rosicrucians*, 1879). Presumably the conventions of his era obliged this early folklorist and learned scholar to avoid stating directly that the 'Most Christian' Order was a pagan cult derived from matriarchal blood and seed symbolism. Anyone with the patience to work through Jennings's comments will find a wealth of information disguised as speculation, much of which has been treated in more open manner by later writers as new research.

The connection between the Order of the Garter and the famous Round Table is nothing less than a restatement of the conquest of Bran by Beli. The 'Holy Grail' extends symbolically to the Celtic or even pre-Celtic 'Cauldron', usually connected with the Goddess Kerridwen. As is suggested by the ritual cutting and cooking of the Wren, in song if not in fact, Bran of the prophetic head was an early native deity whose sacred bird was the wren, and his function was that of a link with the Underworld. This evolved into the Grail myth as the form of vessel became more sophisticated, with numerous origins for the cup itself being drawn into the theme. The myth was of course taken over by Christianity, but the 'Arthur' statement of it is derived from the native hero-cult of Bran while the 'Garter' version is derived from the cult of Beli. Possibly Beli's solar history merged more easily with Christianity than the older Underworld pattern of Bran. It is interesting to find, in a mummers' play collected by Alfred Williams, that the hero is not Saint George, but Arthur O'Bran. This Arthur is the Tanner in a Robin Hood plot and is, of course, defeated in battle. The symbol of Beli in the bird kingdom was the Robin.

A close analysis of the Order of the Garter should reveal further information to support the cult theory, but it is not necessary to subject the evidence to a strictly historical framework. Saint George and the Order, and its national popularity, were more than mere historical regenerations of a mixture of the two national cult-heroes. They show a change of consciousness, a racial evolution of attitude, and a crucial bridging period which set the pattern for the present day. A people's history is not necessarily limited or even decided by the winning and losing of wars, or by the control of trade, but it is deeply linked to their basic 'religious' or inner growth of power images.

The polar alternation of dominance is shown in folksong by the ancient themes usually symbolised as characters. These are not merely the remains of outdated cults, but expressions of shifts of polarity that rule human life. To a lesser degree this expression extends through all forms of folksong and music, as all are derived from the basic magical utterances that were our first vocalised reaction to life. It is no wonder that folk-material has a power that is most difficult to reproduce or to imitate through intellectual contrivance, for folksong, like all inspirations of art and science, is a visionary process that transcends form.

The Keys of Heaven

The 'Dilly Song' is surely the best known and most popular of all true folksongs. It is still widely sung throughout Britain, sometimes from tradition but more generally as a result of the publications of the late nineteenth and early twentieth century, mainly derived from West Country variants. The boys of Eton college sang the variant called *Green grow the Rushes Oh,* and a rather corrupt bawdy version can still be heard as a true folksong at most rugby club singarounds . . ..

> Two, two,
> The same to you!
> How's your father?
> All *right . . .!*

Excluding the vast currency as a group or choral song from printed sources, versions of the song from tradition were widespread. Baring-Gould cites German, Flemish, Scots, Breton, Medieval, Latin, Hebrew, Moravian, Greek and French sources (*Songs of the West*).

Many variants were found in England, and the song is well known in the U.S.A.

Many attempts have been made to interpret the Dilly Song. The usual process has been that of fitting each line forcibly into an orthodox framework and to call any details that do not fit 'corruptions'. Some allowance is usually made for Hebrew influence upon the symbolism, and this gives us a good insight into the effect of childhood conditioning upon research carried out in later life. The song is clearly religious, therefore most researchers conclude that it must be Christian. It obviously contains wild elements, therefore these must be traced to Hebrew influence in the same way as the New Testament follows on from the Old. A simple reading of the known Hebrew text destroys this suggestion completely.

The standard Eton/Boy-scout type of variant has a closer connection with the folk variants of Devon, Somerset or Cornwall, for the Hebrew version is a deliberately orthodox song, resembling the British only in pattern. As this Hebrew text is part of the Service for the Second Night of the Passover, we may assume that it has been adapted from some earlier source, a process common to all formal liturgy. From what source could the Orthodox Hebrew and popular Christian songs have derived? Why, in each quite distinctly separate case, was an acceptable variant tailored from a free source such as is noted in oral tradition? This is the consistent pattern that is found in deliberate adaptation of folk religious or magical sequences into formal authorised worship.

The ritual form of the Dilly songs falls within the type already discussed, the antiphonal group pattern. During the nineteenth century the song was part of chapel-worship in Cornwall, the closest it has come to modern liturgical use, and amateur stage performers were laughed at when they offered Cornish audiences one of their own folk-hymns as a popular entertainment (see Baring-Gould, *Songs of the West*).

The words of the Cornish variants, however, were not those of the light Christian version generally known, but were rather obscure. The puritan chapel-goers were retaining a religious song which was hardly compatible with their general worship, and which was not clear in meaning. This is the hallmark of material that is preserved in a ritualistic manner for some religious reason once known but subsequently lost, and that has reverted from conscious to unconscious use. The Dilly Song is usually interpreted by relating the verses to Biblical characters or incidents, without regard to its actual *structure*, the real clue to its origin. The meaning of the song cannot be revealed by this inadequate type of attempt as there is no original version, and no original religion. The song encompasses several possible religious sources, any of which may have a reasonable and erroneous claim to be the original. Its persistence within oral tradition should have made researchers realise this, but for their conditioning.

To put the Dilly Song into a true context within the folksong and folk-lore, a new method of interpretation is needed. The archetype of the song is an exposition of the Divine Universe through various stages of manifestation. Once this simple fact has been realised, it is easy to understand why varying faiths all have versions of their own, each apparently deriving from early forms which have in common a mystical concept. (For the song text see p. 81).

The song is more likely to be instructional rather than simply devotional, a finer form of the recitation system which only recently degenerated into the learning of multiplication tables. Such mnemonic means were essential in an illiterate society, and it is quite wrong to assume that a non-literate culture had no body of advanced knowledge. The complex material of 'Druid' origin is our own native example of a body of originally unwritten wisdom, much of which has passed into folk imagery.

The ancient standing-stones of Britain appear to have been orientated according to astronomical and seasonal observations, though this does not imply a coherent national system, as they span long periods of historical time and many cultures and races of people. The Druids inherited the lore that developed with these early cultures, and although folk-tradition links them with the stones and circles, we know that Druids were not the builders, and possibly not even the officiators. Evidence for the complexity of early cultures is continually growing, so it is not surprising that traces of quite advanced astronomical or metaphysical lore may be found in folk-material. The creation-pattern suggested by the Dilly Song is a progression common to religious, magical and mystical thought, and should not be related to any specific cult.

To interpret texts from traditional sources, we need to find a body of lore which is essentially oral, and which is a mystical description of the manifestation of the Universe. Information of this sort will open up new interpretations of the Dilly Song, and explain corruptions and juxta-positions of individual verses. Such metaphysical expositions do exist, ranging from ancient Egyptian through to 'modern' Christian and various oriental sources. Additionally there is an enormous amount of 'occult' literature, which is an intellectual fringe of derived material from traditional sources.

For our interpretation, we shall turn to a basically Hebrew source, but not that of the Passover ritual. The Hebrew origin of our source is merely established because the best formulated variants of this body of lore are found in a set of heretical writings, used by Hebrew and Christian mystics, known as the 'Qabalah'. This material was originally oral, the very name meaning from mouth to ear, and was written or symbolised only to give a record of various learned commentaries. The body of Qabalistic lore is a confused mass of folk-lore and apocryphal writings from many sources and races, and not by any means exclusively Jewish. The best known written sources of this lore are Rabbinical interpretations of a pre-literate mystical system, found in repositories of mythology and folk-lore such as the Zohor, Torah, visions of the Prophets, and known to us through the Bible, in both Old and New Testaments. This vast body of lore reduces to a basic tradition, which acts as a broad key to all forms of myth, religion and folk-lore.

No attempt is made here to suggest any intrinsic *religious* value of the Qabalah, or to interpret it as anything other than a body of magical or mystical symbolism which is pan-cultural. By relating this to our native British lore, we benefit by comparing one body of myth to another, but any conclusions are not dependent upon modern or ancient philosophies. These philosophies, which have evolved around the essentially simple Qabalah, are a matter of personal discretion, and not of comparative symbology.

The prime emblem of the Qabalah, and of the Dilly Song, is the TREE OF LIFE (see diagram p. 80). We have commented upon a general use of this symbol in Celtic lore, e.g. the Irish Tree of Wisdom and the little hazel connected with the Gaulish cult of Esus. These in turn can be traced to other tree-cults, well documented in Frazer's and Graves' works. The Qabalistic Tree of Life was not a vegetative symbol, but was a more advanced and magico-mathematical structure based upon a decimal system. It unfolded or manifested in ten clearly defined stages (as does the Cornish Dilly Song) from heaven to earth. Rather than attempt to read our West-country song as a list of vague Biblical attributions, we can now establish its link with the ancient and *systematic* metaphysics.

Considerable argument has developed over fine interpretations of the Tree-of-Life structure and many books—ranging from learned translations to sensational rubbish—have accumulated like parasitic growths upon its stem. No discussion of or reference to these is necessary, as the basic units of the Tree are clearly defined and agreed upon, and these are all that is required.

The following song-texts are used for analysis: the standard text, well known to all; the variant printed in Baring-Gould's *Songs of the West*; a version from the archives of Bristol City Library; and occasional reference to other texts which may be found in the song appendix.

Using the Cornish song as a basic variant, it compares in quite a close manner with the Tree of Life.* (It is not being suggested though, that Cornish people are the lost tribes of Israel, or that British lore is in any way derived from Jewish tradition.) If we proceed from Heaven down to Earth and follow the traditional route of the Fallen Angels, we can compare our unlikely symbolic relatives of song and glyph en route, using the relevant diagrams for reference.

ONE. 'With the exception of some differences in reading, all versions definitely refer to God Almighty.' This pleasantly naive and sturdy Christian statement sets the tone for an English Folk Dance and Song Society leaflet entitled 'The Mystery of Green Grow the Rushes Oh', based on the standard text and standard readings. Regrettably, the title is the closest we ever get to the mystery of the song.

'One is One and All Alone and Ever More shall be so' sang the Cornish fishermen. If these terms were translated into Hebrew, we would find that they were Names of God. In a famous Qabalistic document *The Sepher Yetzirah* we may read 'The One is Only One, and has no Second, and before One, how can you count?'. Each *mishnah* or verse of this work is preceded by the line 'there are ten intangible Sephiroth' (spheres of evolution or creation). Now there are ten stages of the Dilly Song, for variants with twelve verses represent a merging of decimal metaphysics with another system discussed later.†

The first Sphere of the Tree of Life is that of the original creative power of existence, a refined concept (NOT identified with God Almighty, which the Qabalah links to the second Sphere). This is the ancient deity

---

*Some sources for Qabalistic literature are listed in the Bibliography
†See also *Hymn of Jesus* in song appendix (p. 124).

of the breathing of origination, whose Biblical name is not Jehovah or Yahwe, but 'I am that I am'. An exhaustive study of God-names can be found in numerous reference works, but only part of this abstruse subject is relevant to our folksong.

'One is God the Righteous Man who sent our souls to rest, AMEN'. This uses several religious terms, or god-names, and the word *Amen* is always connected with the first sphere of the Tree, meaning the-end-is-in-the-beginning, a typical mystical concept. At verse ten, the Dilly Song says 'Ten forgives all kinds of sin, from ten begin again Oh'. The tenth sphere of the Tree of Life was regarded as being symbolically and metaphysically an opposite or complimentary reflection of the first; 'Kether (The first) is in Malkuth (The tenth) after a different fashion' (see diagram).

TWO. 'Two of them are lily-white boys clothed all in Green Oh.' This immediately reveals links with *The Two Brothers*, but Baring-Gould surprisingly suggests that the 'lily-white boys' are the astrological sign of Gemini. In old calendar terms the Sun entered Gemini at the beginning of May, the time of the pagan Beltane feast. The possibility of developing an astrological implication from the song is tempting, especially with those variants having 12 verses, yet these versions were more probably built up to suit Christian adaptation. The twelvefold system adapted by the Christian cult, however, was used to fit Apostles to earlier patterns which had astrological links. We are dealing here with a *synthetic* type of thought, which continually returns to a state or stage where systems such as music, mathematics, astrology and general imagery merge into one another. There is no contradiction in the Dilly Song even though we find it temporarily jumping from one type of symbolism to another, for it is still fulfilling its pattern of exposition, be it pagan or Christian.

In Mishnah 10 of *The Sepher Yetzirah* we find 'TWO: Air from Spirit'. Gemini is an 'Airy Sign', of course, so perhaps Baring-Gould's inference, drawn from an early work on festal embroidery, is correct. The Second Sphere of the Tree of Life is said to be that of the Unity of Being, expressed in the First Sphere, now divided into action, into that of Doing, making 1 into 2. This is called the sphere of Wisdom. A great deal was made in early mathematics of the relationship between the numobersne to four, which add sequentially to ten. It is interesting to recall that the symbol of Cornwall is not much different from the Pythagorean tetractys—a pyramid of ten dots (One for All, and All for One!). Ten was said to be the perfect number, as it was the sum of 1–4 reverting to its unity 1(0). We shall not expand upon this difficult art here, but it does reveal itself within the folksong. We can see why this second stage is also called 'God's own son' or 'Christ's natures' in

The Lailly Worm, *or serpent coiled round the Tree of Life*

some song-texts. Rather than delve into the murky depths of classified heresy, we can merely add that the reading of the Two Boys as Christ and John the Baptist is a rather unfortunate—though common— explanation of the second verse. It leads us into the whole issue of God, Father and Son, which caused so many heads to roll, including that of John the Baptist. That incident may well indicate the customary pattern that a priest or prophet was expected to die after he had handed on his power to his successor. John, of course, was a typical other-world seer, after the fashion of our native 'Bran' cult, while his divine successor Jesus was clearly a solar figure, after the nature of 'Beli'.

The Qabalistic attributes of Wisdom to this second stage or sphere links up well with the line 'Two was the jury' from the Bristol variant, and the lily-white babes or maids are typical images to personify wisdom.

THREE. Are the Rivals. Three of them are Strangers, Three is Eternity. These lines may not seem to be compatible—but they are

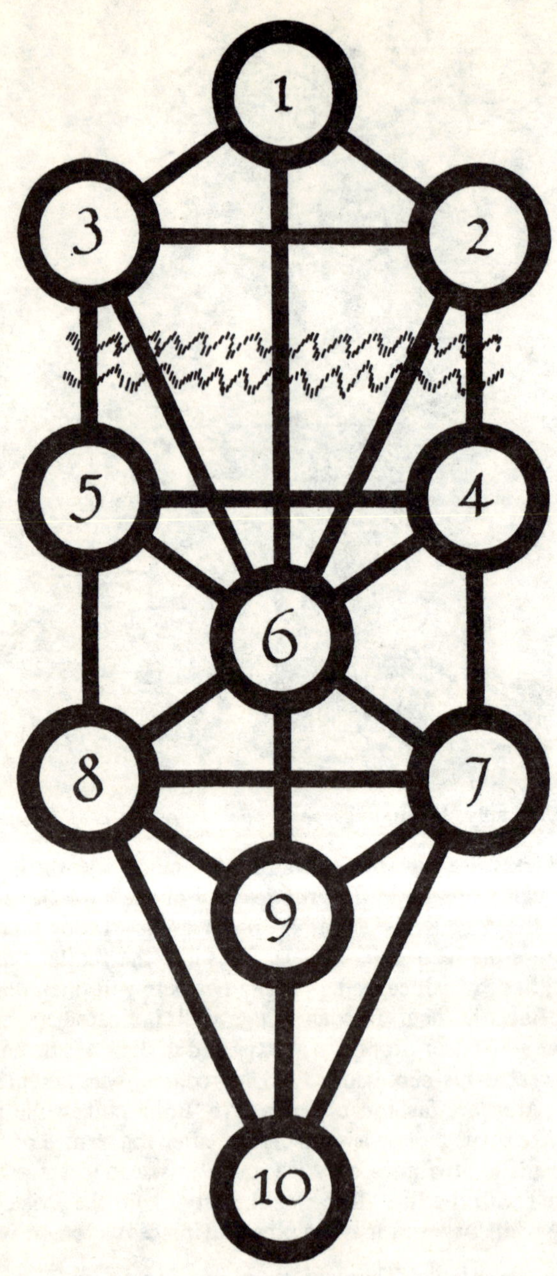

The 'Tree of Life' as a mathematical symbol

1. Crown, Origin. (Kether in Hebrew) Uranus
2. Wisdom, Almighty God (Chockmah. Heb) Neptune
3. Understanding, the Great Mother (Binah) Saturn
4. Mercy. The All Giver (Chesed) Jupiter
5. Severity. The All Restrictor (Jivurah) Mars
6. Beauty. The SON of Light (Tiphareth) The Sun
7. Victory. The Young Goddess (Netzach) Venus
8. Glory. The Young God (Hod) Mercury
9. Foundation. The Life Mother (Yesod) Luna
10. Kingdom. The Earth Mother (Malkuth) Earth

One of them is all alone and ever more shall be so
Two of them are lily-white boys all clothed all in green Oh
Three of them are strangers o'er the wide world they are rangers
Four it is the Dilly Hour when blooms the Gilly Flower
Five it is the Dilly Bird that's seldom seen but heard
Six is the Ferryman in the boat that o'er the River floats oh
Seven are the Seven Stars in the Sky, the Shining Stars be Seven Oh
Eight it is the Morning's break when all the World's awake Oh
Nine it is the pale Moonshine, the Shining Moon is Nine Oh
Ten Forgives all kinds of Sin, from Ten begin again Oh

---

connected in the concept of the Tree and of Numbers. The Third Sphere of the Tree of Life is that of Understanding and also that of Eternity, the Mother deep of Time and Space. The EFDSS reminds us correctly, in their leaflet, that rivals were originally partners, as in earlier uses of the word, then refers us directly to the Holy Trinity. Be ye far from here, oh ye profane folklorists! The Great Mother has been removed from her place within the Holy Trinity, but upon the older Tree of Life she remains as 'Mara' (Mary) the infinite Sea of Sorrows, the womb and tomb of all existence. The mystical origin of matter and the fall into creation are linked with the nature of this Third Sphere, and the strangers ranging o'er the wide world are relatives of fallen man, expelled from the Garden. The Garden of Eden is clearly a Qabalistic myth which has been altered to suit the transfer from matriarchy to patriarchy. The basic heresy of the Qabalah and of related gnostic sects was that they openly retained the status of the Great Mother. Orthodox Christianity was forced to return to her in secret, as we have seen from the analysis of Saint George.

The magical significance of the number 3 is that of a step taken which has to be worked through in full before it may be nullified. The same concept applies to variant lines such as 'Three are the Strivers'. The linguistic athletics of the rivals are no longer necessary to justify the unbalanced sexuality of the Christian Trinity.

FOUR. The Gospel Preachers, the Gospel Makers, the Four Evangelists, and the Dilly Hour when blooms the Gilly Flower. Four was the Open Door.

The progression to Four Evangelists is consistent with our magical-religious unfolding of the Cosmos. The symbols for the Evangelists, still seen in stained-glass windows and carved upon fonts and altars, are the Eagle, the Lion, the Man, and the Bull. These were adapted from an older system where they were the signs for the Four Elements of Creation—Air, Fire, Water and Earth. After the gestation in the Womb of the Third Sphere, the creation process crosses the Abyss (see diagram) which exists between the upper three Spheres and the rest of the Tree. This is the gap between supernal principles of power and the actual manifestation of energies. The four elements were said to be the basis of all patterns of energy and creation in expression. The Fourth Sphere is usually termed that of 'mercy' or 'bounty', a positive flowing-out of creative power. Four is an open door, and not merely for convenience of rhyme.

The concept of the Elements or Evangelists is linked with the 'Circled Cross' pattern (seen on many ancient stone crosses and carvings) which disposes the powers around the circles of the seasons. The Tree of Life was actually supposed to grow within the Garden, which was laid out after the pattern of a Quartered Circle with the Tree growing in the Centre (see associated diagram).

The *Sepher Yetzirah* or Book or Formation says at this point, 'He engraved out and hewed out the Throne of Glory, Fiery Angels and *Ophanim* (wheels, literally), and Holy Beings, and Ministering Angels'. These are all angelic orders connected with the mechanics of divine creation, later assimilated by the Evangelists, Apostles, Saints and other Christian images. The early Church, it should be noted, utilised the angelic orders in its thought, as is still done in monastic practice today.

St Thomas Aquinas, when describing the analogy between physical and spiritual life, uses the same Qabalistic terms that relate to our Dilly Song: 'Now in the movement of bodies the more perfect and primary ones have position.

'Therefore the principal spiritual operations are described under this appearance' (this refers to the concepts of the Supernal Spheres of the Tree of Life), 'They are three different movements, for instance, circular, whereby anything is moved uniformly around its centre; next is straight, according to which a thing proceeds from one to another; and the third is serpentine, which is made up of both circular and straight'. These definitions are exactly those of the Angelic Orders mentioned in the extract above from the Book of Formation (see *Summa Secunda Secundae Quest*; clxxx, Art vi vid. Appendix Latine— as quoted in Father G. B. Chambers, *Folk Song, Plainsong*).

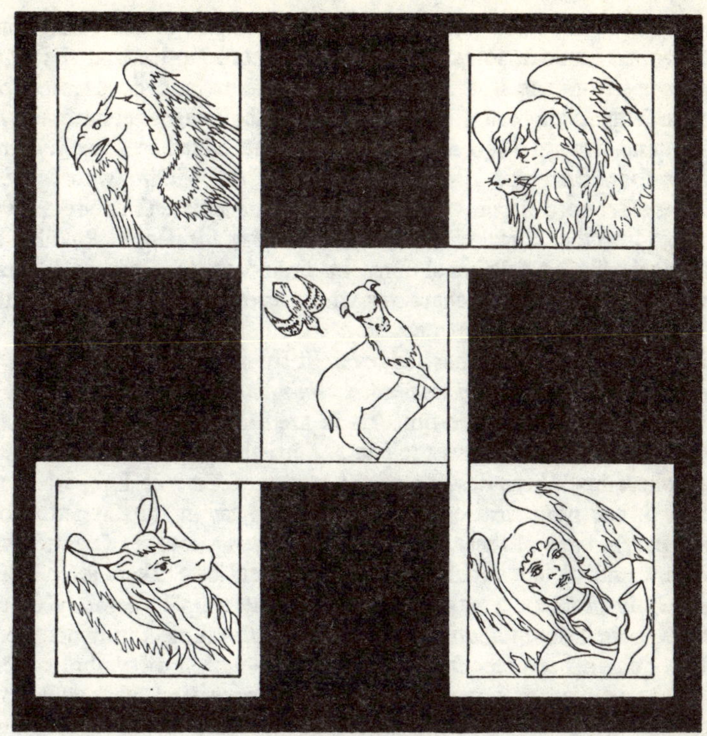

The Four Beasts

The beautiful line from Cornwall about the Dilly Hour and the Gilly Flower should remain a mystery inviolate, and any attempt to penetrate its veil of folk lyricism would be an act of pedantic sacrilege.

It has been suggested several times that the word Dilly may be derived from the Welsh DILLYN, meaning pretty or gay, and the Welsh DILLYNION, meaning bright jewels. This interpretation originated with Baring-Gould. The Tree of Life, curiously, is often described as Ten Jewels, or Ten Lights. This same Tree appears in the carol *Leaves of Life*, with Seven Virgins sitting under it. The Serpent coiled around the Tree, found in the ballad *The Lailly Worm*, is not only the Serpent of the Garden of Eden, and the Dragon of Saint George, but also the Great Serpent upon the Tree of Life whose folds rise 'even unto the Abyss'. The convolutions of this worm represent the paths of connection between the Spheres, or the pattern of power that links the fallen beings to the divine worlds.

This same Tree is found again in *Thomas the Rhymour* (see also p. 131), who offers to pluck its forbidden fruit for the Fairy Queen. As she undoubtedly knew her Qabalah, being the Goddess of the Other-world, she warned him not to eat of it as it was fatal. Notice that she warns him away from the fruit in the pagan variants, and does not attract him to it as in the usual interpretation of the images, connected with Adam and Eve. In *The Leaves of Life*, Christ, nailed to a big yew tree, suffers for Adam and Eve. He is, in fact, the Victim who is hung upon the Tree of Life, and who is supposed to mediate the divine powers through into the mortal world for the benefit of his people. Possibly the 'Thomas' of this folk-carol may be linked to the famous Thomas Rhymour, an historical character whose prophecies were still printed until early in the nineteenth century.

It cannot be over-emphasised, even at the risk of repetition, that we are looking briefly at a *manner of conceptualising*, and not at a specific system of cosmic interpretation. There are at least two cosmic schemes within the Dilly Song, plus their later Christian accretions. The first is the Sphere-by-Sphere descent of the standard Tree of Life, while the second is the numerical computation of 1–4, as in the Circled Cross. The exact linkage of these two glyphs has been a source of centuries of constant and violent argument between would-be Seekers after Peace. The whole problem is easily resolved by the simple geometry of any given sphere in mathematics, but this is not the subject in hand.

It is quite absurd to demand any strict definition of symbol systems as they are merely working analogies of processes of thought and intuition. Throughout the centuries people have believed that such symbols lead to an awareness that is higher or better than straight-line logic, everyday disordered thinking. Whether this is true or not, these areas of consciousness do exist, and are expressed by the kind of image under discussion.

FIVE. Is the dilly bird that's seldom seen but heard! Five is the symbol at your door, or at your feet, and five is a man alive. Occasionally five is the ferryman in the boat, but this is probably a juxtaposition of SIX, as will be seen later.

The Fifth Sphere of the Tree of Life is that of Severity, linked to Mars. The magical power of the pentagram, or five-pointed star, associated with the 'symbol at your door', is well known, though few people have bothered to explain its significance. It is the shape of a man standing upright with arms outstretched. The Qabalah uses this symbol to suggest that a fifth element of divinity, present in man, may control or discipline the Elements. We see here whence Christ surrounded by the Four Evangelists developed. Five is the symbol of restraint, supposed to banish demons. This is simply because it is linked in the ancient symbolism to the Fifth Sphere, where Seraphim with fiery swords purge away evil. From here it degenerated into common magic, wherein powerful entities are supposed to be at the mercy of the Medieval wizard, to divulge great wealth, or to captivate desirable virgins. The symbol need not be sought far from home, for it is one of those displayed in the English Sword Dance, woven out of interlocking swords.

These sword dances are undoubtedly magical in origin, as has been pointed out by Violet Alford in her thorough work *Sword Dance and Drama*. The patterns of these weaving dances are actually those of cosmic evolution, expressed in a similar way to that of the Dilly Song. Original expressions of the old Mysteries would have involved both dance and song, linked to cosmic exposition.

The 'Dilly' bird which perches upon the Tree of Life may be seen as a cult-bird, such as the woodpecker or the cuckoo, which are both seldom seen but heard; but it is more likely that the 'Dillies' and 'Gillies' are rhyming whimsy, derived from other words now lost. The same sort of non-sense is common in folksong choruses and mouth-music to fill musical phrases, while corrupt lines in folksongs are retained with no reference or concern for their lack of meaning (see, for example, Little Suzy and her hoppers with silver strings, already mentioned in *The Two Brothers*, where hoppers is a corruption of harping. See also a corruption of 'Merry Lincoln' into 'American corn', C. J. Sharp: 'Sir Hugh of Lincoln notes', FSFS, and many others).

SIX. Is the Ferryman in the Boat that o'er the River floats Oh. Six is a Crucifix, six for the six proud walkers.

The Ferryman is familiar to us by now, as Saint George, as Edward, and all their predecessors. Even Baring-Gould was bold enough to identify him with Charon, the classical Ferryman of Souls. The Sixth Sphere is linked with the SUN or the Principle of Harmony and Beauty. In Celtic tradition the Sun was said to be the sum of the blazing souls of ancestors in paradise.

This is the realm of the Saviour (Six was the Crucifix) and of the Archangel Michael, whose place in myth has already been touched upon. The ancient Sacrificial King operated spiritually from this Sixth Sphere as a mediator of the power of the Mother Goddess. Christ, the son of God, should be positively identified here with all the other Sons of Light through the ages, and by analogy with the sun of our solar system around which the planets revolve. Nowadays this concept could also be applied to the structure of the atom, and still hold good.

The Sepher Yetzirah gives SIX as 'He sealed the Abyss, He turned downward and sealed it with YVH'. This YVH is part of the Holy Name of God, reputed to have magical powers, but actually a scientific codification of metaphysics. The Abyss is that great unknown gap between Heaven and Earth, the River which the Dead have to cross, spanned by the razor-edged bridge of fairy lore, or crossed by the vessel of the Ferryman.

The Six Proud Walkers, of course, do not fit this central theme, this fulcrum of the Powers of the Tree. They are derived from the song *The Joys of Mary*, which has had some influence in the substitution of other verses into the Dilly song. It is a composed attempt at replacing the pagan numerical song with something more acceptable. We ought to reject the notion, voiced again by the EFDSS, that 'there can be no doubt that the reference is to the six water-pots used in the miracles of Cana of Galilee'. Alas, cultural conditioning is showing again, and there can be no doubt that these six pots of miraculous wine, borrowed from Mithras, were served to the happy guests at the feast by the six proud waiters mentioned in some American variants of the song.

SEVEN. Is the Crown of Heaven, or the Seven Stars in the Sky. The term 'Crown' was usually the name for the First Sphere upon the Tree of Life, but the Crown of Shining Stars was more likely to be the Pleiades, a constellation often given mystical significance. The Goddess has a crown of seven stars which might also be the seven planets of the solar system, and the 7th Sphere is linked to Venus and Victory or Achievement. The Archangel of this Sphere is Auriel, who was said to wear a Crown bearing a precious stone that fell from Heaven, sometimes rumoured to be set in the Holy Grail. We are reminded here of the various meteoric sacred stones that are given religious significance, and of the heaven-sent metals which Miss Alford suggests inspired the sword dances mentioned above.

The Seven Keys of Heaven of the Bristol variant, or 'seven was the Gate of Heaven' is usual terminology for the Seven Lower Spheres upon the Tree of Life, also represented as Seven Gates to be negotiated in one's attempt to reach immortality. These are shown as the Druidic realms of the Other-world, which the heroes of the 'Spoils of Annwm' had to pass through in their search for the cauldron.

EIGHT. The Great Archangel, The Eight Archangels, The April Rainers, and Eight it is the Mornings' break when all the world's awake Oh. This last beautiful line of poetry gives us yet another surprising link out of apparent fancy which only makes sense within the cosmic interpretation of the song. The Eight Sphere, that of Glory, is linked to the Archangel Raphael. He is the Keeper of the Gates of Dawn, and his angels—the *Bene Elohim*—are the 'inspirers' who create new horizons within the intellect of mankind.

It has been suggested that eight Archangels pose a problem, but there are no less than Ten Archangels upon the Tree of Life. As Raphael is an Archangel bearing a Sword, we may be reading the common confusion between Raphael/Michael/Saint George. In representations of these figures their attributes are often exchanged. The Great Archangel is usually Michael, but the Archangel of the Eighth Sphere is properly Raphael, although the two have been juxtaposed in some Qabalistic writings. Many carvings of Michael show him with a Sword, which is incorrect, as he is traditionally the Spear- or Lance-bearer.

'Eight it was a landscape' is not open to mystical interpretation, but is good poetry within the song.

NINE. It is the Pale Moonshine. All versions agree upon this in one form or another. The Ninth Sphere is that of Foundation, and of Luna, the ancient Goddess of fecundity, of death and birth . . . of that part of the other-world closest to our earth. The period of human gestation is usually nine months, while the flow of tides and of menstruation is literally governed by the moon's phases.

The term 'Nine Bright Shiners' is interesting, as the angels of the Ninth Sphere are the *Aishim*, or 'brightly shining ones'. These beings supervise the mechanics of transporting souls in and out of their bodies during birth and death.*

TEN. Forgives or forbids all kinds of sin—*from Ten begin again Oh*. This could almost be a line from a Qabalistic verse or commentary, did we not know that it derives from a traditional Cornish song. The Tenth Sphere is the Kingdom of the World, from which souls begin their long climb back to heaven. The vision of Jacob's ladder is nothing more nor less than a representation of the Tree of Life. The Tenth Sphere is the product of the emanations of the preceding nine, and the Great Mother of Earth is the true forgiver of sins. She offers all created beings equal opportunity to die and to be reborn in new forms. The

---

*In a Dorset variant of the song we find 'Nine are the Gabriel rangers'. The Archangel Gabriel is always regent of the 9th Sphere, in the Qabalah. It should be remembered that Gabriel was closely connected with the Virgin Mary, and her magical conception. The Gospel according to Saint Luke informs us that both Mary and Elizabeth, John the Baptist's mother, conceived miraculously, through the mediation of the Archangel Gabriel. Both these ladies were 'of the daughters of Aaron', whose miraculous Rod of Power should be connected with the Spear of Archangel Michael, and all other such implements. Gabriel was said in folklore to carry the The Wild Hunt, with his Gabriel Hounds.

Again we find evidence of the belief in a two-way passage between the inner and outer Worlds, by which both life and death powers and human souls were able to travel.

line of the song suggests reincarnation, a concept familiar to the Qabalah, and also originally accepted by the Christian Church, though later deemed heretical. The Celtic people seem to have believed in some form of reincarnation, but the beliefs attributed to the Druids are confused upon this issue and it is not clear whether they accepted reincarnation proper, or transmigration or metempsychosis. They may have had a system of combined processes, as is suggested by Lewis Spence (see *Mysteries of Britain*, etc.).

The Ten Commandments of course, belong here, both as Christian and Hebraic rules of primitive conduct within the ordinary world. These were superseded by the Saviour, who brought back a new way of conduct from the Divine Realms, as was expected of him, and as was attempted by all his spiritual ancestors (The Sermon on the Mount).

The numbers eleven and twelve, as suggested, derive from another system and were probably added to bring the decimal song into line with Christian practice.

'Eleven are the Eleven that went to Heaven' is not merely a reference to the Apostles minus Judas Iscariot. It links up with the crossing of the Abyss, an eleventh area (not a sphere) which bridges this gap left by the Fall into Matter. The hole is said to be gradually closing as we evolve back into the Divine Plan of Perfection. There is also a complicated argument connected with the origin of the signs of the Zodiac, which may have been ten in number at one time, but were later further divided. What is more probable is that tenfold and twelvefold systems evolved spontaneously, as the magical images themselves did, without a great deal of regard for historical events. Twelve, therefore, for the Twelve Apostles is quite reasonably connected, due to the Zodiac signs that they absorbed during their growth to superiority in the Western world.

The Bristol variants of the Dilly Song were kindly sent to the author by Mr John Shaw. The first text was originally performed in the Barton Hill Mummer's Play, quite an important connection, as these plays are expressions of the pagan religious theme. The song was collected by F. C. Jones. The second variant was collected by Mr Shaw from a Mrs Hinchcliffe, of Thornbury, who learned it as a child from her grand-mother in the North of England. She volunteered this childhood song, almost forgotten, after hearing Mr Shaw perform the Barton Hill song on local television. Such is the devious path of oral tradition! Both texts are similar to *The Joys of Mary*, a parallel Christianised form of the Dilly Song, which has a style suggestive of composition rather than evolution. This particular song, collected in various parts of Britain, has exercised a strong influence on the Dilly Song in cases where words have been forgotten.

Divergence from West Country texts and others is also due to the poetical replacement of meanings that are in doubt, but certain keys within the version given here do show affinity with some system now lost. (See page 124 for this text.)

'Twelve was the Gates of Hell' is quite contrary to the usual reading of Twelve Apostles. If we count downwards on the Tree of Life, and allow eleven for the bridging of the Abyss, twelve is the number *below* that of the mortal world. Traditionally this world was said to be the nearest to Hell.

The use in these texts of Eleven as the Crown of Heaven may also be more than mere rhyme convenience, as the fallen Crown is supposed to be restored to its rightful place by the return across the Abyss.

'Ten was a golden Pen/Lions Den' are obvious replacement rhymes, substitutes for other attributions.

'Nine was the Glass of Wine' is transferred from *The Joys of Mary*, perhaps, and Mrs Hinchcliffe also replaced some of her forgotten words from the Barton Hill version performed by Mr Shaw.

'Four was a lady's birth' is possibly a corruption, yet it is not a rhyme substitution, so stands apart from the other lines.

One wonders how many people alive today can still remember odd verses to this mystical song learned in their early childhood?

The brief and broadly based comparisons made above are mere indications of the origin of the Dilly Song; an accurate and detailed study could be attempted only by considering variants in all languages, and tracing the linguistic roots of their eccentricities. All variants follow the evolution pattern, decimal or duodecimal, and are connected with ancient sacred number-systems supposed to reveal the metaphysics of existence. The similarity may even be extended Eastwards, where the Dilly Song has strong affinities with the I CHING.

So common are the symbolic links that it is impossible to leave this subject without briefly mentioning a connection between our song, folk symbolism in general, and the Tarot images. Despite the pseudo-mystical and fortune-telling nonsense that has accumulated around them, the Tarot symbols are identical in many respects to those of our folksongs and tales. These ancient picture-cards, of unknown origin, are from the same region of deep mass-consciousness as folksong, hence their perpetual fascination. The sets of pictures in existence at present show the racial images with varying degrees of clarity, although a few modern versions have departed from the power of the group-unconscious into speculative realms of awareness known only to the designer, based upon intellectual schemes and theories or upon the influence of drugs—usually a guarantee of failure.

Most interesting in our present context are images made in the

*'Six is the Ferryman in the boat
that o'er the river floats Oh'*

early part of this century by the researcher A. E. Waite, who drew on traditional sources and attempted to produce a set of cards which formed a bridge between those rapidly becoming stylised beyond recognition, and the fruits of his own work with various streams of linguistic and original research into ancient lore.

The verses of the Dilly Song will be found scattered through this highly colourful pack, each of which is a full picture-image. It would be interesting to learn if Waite deliberately included the Cornish Dilly Song in his designs, or if the ancient roots merely re-grew in a national style when he set out to correct the cards.

The Tarot symbols are probably more useful in exploring the structures of areas that are usually non-aware or unconscious, than for their traditional and trivial derivative of fortune-telling. In addition to the complete Dilly song, scattered from suite to suite and verse to verse, several other magical folksong images will be clearly seen in a pack of these cards. The song itself must have had such enormous popular currency that it could not be kept out of worship by decree, and so was 'converted'. The related mumming-plays and seasonal rites were sternly opposed, yet never successfully suppressed. The 'evil'

Tarot cards were merely pictorial representations of the same forces shown in the plays and songs, and told the same eternal story. Possibly the pictures were at one time related to the old oral tradition of worship, as were the Ikons used in Eastern Christianity. The pagan worship-system was banned and suppressed, so the images passed into the folk-tradition. Only in recent years have the Tarot emerged from anonymity into the glamour of 'occultism', where writers and practitioners forget that no 'secret' body of knowledge is required to account for the images present in the mind of mankind, and that 'magical' orders were open for all in folksong and ceremonies throughout the centuries.

Musical Considerations

Most folksong analysis and commentary has been confined to the study of texts. The weight of evidence for any theory about pagan beliefs in folksong usually lies with an interpretation or explanation of the words and their symbolism. The music itself, the airs of traditional songs, generally receives less direct attention. After notation and collection, most of the work done with folk-music has been classification, often carried to extreme detail, as in the modal theory of B. H. Bronson's *Traditional Tunes for the Child Ballads*. Beyond the usual admission that folk-melodies are very beautiful and at times rich, very little information has been deduced from the music itself.

It is usually accepted, due to an immense accumulation of error, that folk-melodies are cast in 'ancient modes'. This misleading concept has a long history, and is actually quite meaningless. It simply suggests that songs which are not obviously music-hall or modern pieces, such as Victorian popular songs, have a definite pre-harmonic, and essentially melodic form. These folk-melodies are often lovely and polished; primitive, yet very subtle, and seldom dull. In fact the whole issue of modes in folksong is very confused because of, rather than in spite of, numerous efforts to clarify it. Most works include an individual terminology and definition, and there are numerous unrelated attempts to force folksong into the categories of classical musicology and the 'Greek' modes. An unsuspecting reader of experts in the folk-music field is likely to endure a long and hard wrestling-bout with terminology, and even the musically literate reader will find the subject confused by many willing hands. This welter of terminology, created solely for purposes of classification, but gradually grown into an end in itself, can be cleared up quite easily.

A mode is merely a progression or path between two points. In music the points are differently pitched noises. Any group of notes may be said to be a mode, if an arbitrary order is put upon them. Definition occurs when three or more steps or intervals are set in directed order, ranging from lower to higher pitch. The common names and terms for pitches, intervals notes and the like are quite irrelevant to this definition. Most of the problems created over 'modal' music have been unsuccessful attempts to relate patterns of notes to formal musical terms, rather than use the natural order or development which is, of course, the opposite way round.

The use of 'scales' or ascending and descending definitions of pitch-patterns is quite natural to the human vocal and mental apparatus. Traditional singers were never aware of singing in modes, ancient or modern—they merely sang. The same melody would be noted in differing modes from different singers, or even from the same singer, and the general implication is that genuine folk-singers who relied entirely on the oral tradition for their music retained melody by its *shape*, or contour, rather than as an aggregation of notes, intervals and phrases. The singers with whom Cecil Sharp and other collectors in England worked reproduced their songs in a wholly non-conscious fashion; as a rule they could not sing a melody without the words that were associated with it. If a melody was sung back to them, but in a different mode, many singers would make no distinction between the new variant and the original. Later evidence, such as that of Sharp in the United States, suggests that this musical unawareness in the descendants of the English peasants was a symptom of the tradition atrophying. The Anglo-Celtic settlers of the Southern Appalachian mountains, living in very primitive conditions and having none of the artistic or social benefits found close to the English labourer, were more musically aware. They could sing melodies without words, and comment and improvise consciously within the framework of the oral tradition. As the music collected in this area revealed a great deal of exciting and apparently 'early' material, Sharp maintained that it represented the English tradition (though a more accurate term would have been British) in a healthier state of survival.

The practice of singing 'modally' indicates that folk-music is our closest link with the music of the almost unrecorded past. It is retained within an astonishingly accurate tradition, yet at the same time has been constantly regenerated by a continuous racial process of experience and experiment. From this process evolved all early music, and native musics of any sort. It might be supposed that we could apply our knowledge of ancient music possibly in religious use, and see how such forms compare with folksong. Unfortunately our actual knowledge of such music is very small and open to various forms of misinterpretation. To attempt to reach back to early music, we have to travel via—folksong.

'Traditional' music is the clearest record of what early music may have been like. International study of folk-music can still reveal information from cultures in many differing stages of development. This does not imply that particular folksongs will give specific examples of early musical forms, but that the approach to music through an oral method, and the general form defined by the nature of the human voice and hands, will be similar. The commonly termed 'Greek modes' are the patterns of notes most natural to the human voice. The relationships between these intervals today have been deliberately altered to suit certain instruments and conventions of harmony. The modes as presented upon the keyboard are not strictly the modes in which we naturally sing, but are a tempered approximation of them. Furthermore, most of our modern sensitivity to music and individual singing is wholly conditioned by these alterations, and by harmonic concepts. Such concepts were non-existent in early music, and are still non-existent in Western folk-music, other than through formal influence.

It is a great mistake to assume that because folk-music is melodic, not harmonic, that it is simple or trivial. The folk-music that we have record of today is melodically complex, and the evidence from Ireland, Scotland and possibly Wales, strongly suggests that our native music is the remnant of a very advanced system. This system had its own forms, styles and conventions, such as are still found in some Eastern 'classical' musics which have never evolved a harmonic form.

It is too easy to assume that because Western art-music has developed a peak of harmonic style and sophistication that it is the leading form of music altogether.

Folk-music itself is an all-inclusive and quite indiscriminate collection of songs and tunes. It includes recent comedy entertainments side-by-side with ancient magical ballads, with every type of material in between, often within the mind of any one singer. What is significant is that the ancient ballads survive the passage of time, whereas the popular entertainments do not. Where are the pop-songs of the eighteenth century? They have not grown into folksongs, as one might expect. It is rare to come across one of the thousands of bawdy songs, such as those in Thomas D'Urfey's 'Pills to Purge Melancholy or Mirth and Wit', whereas recent bawdy songs, usually of lower quality, are quite common. The trivia of popular entertainment seem to be taken up and cast away as lightly as they are produced, but the vital images of the tradition of the West have greater endurance. Romantic broadsheets and songs and those of a semi-historical or moral nature have a longer currency, usually stretching back a century or so, though this is neces-sarily a simplification of the overall picture. Songs have also passed in and out of print, to and from the oral storehouse, into broadsheet, chapbook, and even early song-collections. We should bear in mind the cautionary tale of the recent folksong collector, who claims that an old lady in Somerset said 'Oh, you means they songs that that fellow with the bicycle taught my mother, eh?' Cecil Sharp toured Somerset on a bicycle collecting folksongs, later arranged and published in several volumes.

When we look for possible early *music* in folksong, the process has to be one of weeding out. Obvious popular material can easily be distinguished, though curious examples such as *The Two Magicians* may be found set to music-hall airs. Within the mass of extant folksongs various influences both poetical and musical may be traced, with actual magical ballads and songs forming a nucleus for examination. It is usually in this last group that we find 'ancient' forms of melody, but this is not a strict rule. Many printed songs have been wedded to archaic and beautiful airs, possibly at the expense of whatever words were discarded in their favour. That is no solution to the problem of the apparent antiquity of many folk-melodies and the relatively modern style of their texts. Should we assume that for every broadside song recovered to an old-style melody, an old-style set of words has been lost? It is more likely that the modal melodies are part of a racial repertoire which is both remembered and handed down, and spontaneously regenerated as required. Undoubtedly we have lost song-texts which have been replaced by dreary hack verses, but these may have been nothing more than earlier popular songs in their turn. The folk have a process by which the most banal of songs can be transformed into a beautiful lyric—they simply forget the boring parts.

The musical inheritance has survived where commercial texts have not. If we define folk-music as being the expression of the racial soul, then this is only to be expected, and the form of the melodies themselves will long outlast whatever passing stories are set to them. The exceptions to this are the ritualistic or magical ballads and songs, which have been handed down in a surprisingly good state of preservation, defying time, changes of language and social history with the same ruthless inevitability that their characters display in action.

There is a bridge between ancient music now 'lost', and folksong, now extinct in Britain. This form combines the methods of both, elevated to an extreme peak of beauty and control. As we might expect, this only link between present and past found outside our folk-tradition is well established and carefully guarded within the Church. The link is, of course, Plainsong.

At one time it was a fashionable theory that folk-music was the degraded result of the illiterate peasantry copying courtly music . . . where else could the clods have picked up inspiration? Similarly it was, and occasionally still is, believed that *modal* melodies were copied from Christian liturgical use. In fact actual evidence, to say nothing of common sense, shows that Plainsong derives from folk-music—as does all music of any sort.

The fact that Plainsong was derived from vocal forms *already in use* among the early faithful, who were but recently converted from paganism, has been convincingly demonstrated by the late Father G. B. Chambers in his excellent work *Folksong-Plainsong*. This short book is of enormous value to the folk-lorists and musicologists, especially as it provided references and sources not easily traced by the student outside the cloister. As we might expect, Father Chambers has consistently omitted a rather important factual link in his presentation, although it is clear from his writing that he was well aware of its existence. The music of plainchant was derived from folk-sources, but en route it matured through the existing music of the pagan faiths. As the forms, images and practices of the native cults were steadily absorbed into the Catholic Church, so must the pagan music in worship have been taken up. Texts and names were obviously altered to suit the new religion, though these were not *written*, but orally-transmitted renderings of the Gospel, the new revelation of a new god. The forms were certainly adapted from existing chants, as Father Chambers' carefully accumulated evidence shows.

It remained for the images to be passed into folksong in later years, and to live until quite recently as a body of ritual practices, poetry and music, hardly touched by formal state religion of any sort. The actual music developed not only as a native tradition, and as a courtly art that atrophied with the collapse of classicism, but also as a third stream of intellectual, emotional and spiritual development of expression, the ecclesiastical chant.

The evidence for this inheritance of pagan music tradition is clear. Chambers cites various authorities, including Sextus Pompeius Festus, Lucius Apuleius, Marcus Terrentius Varro, St. Hilary, St Cyril of Alexandria, and admits 'In these quotations classical usage is carried forward, and in a sense consolidated in ecclesiastical custom and becomes part of the Catholic tradition. It therefore forms contact with the great classical tradition of drama and its sources, the original dance and song of the people surrounding the fertility rites and worship of remote ages.' We must realise that these 'remote ages' were exactly the period of Christian evolution, and were directly contemporary with the first Christian missionaries to the West.

Despite the arid period of Roman State worship when people were expected to put their faith in political and quite unsatisfactory gods, much as in the present day, the native or Druid cults were still active in Britain.

In the West of England, pagan traditions survived longer than in the East as actual religions rather than as folk-customs. When we examine Welsh and Irish lore we come across the famous magical power of the Druid bards both in legend and in early history. It is unlikely that their strict years of training and discipline produced nothing more than unsophisticated grunting.

If plainsong is indeed based upon the natural jubilation or inspired expressions of primitive peoples, we must realise that *all* religious music comes from this same source; and its use in worship was by no means the unique property or inspiration of the early Fathers. It is so easy to forget that early people did not in any way separate their religion from daily life. All music, song and dance was, and still essentially is, religious. The split between formal faith and living experience is the sign of a dead religion, not of a developed one.

The Church inherited the science and the experienced practitioners of ancient chant and song. No music of any sort suddenly appears out of nothing, and religious music especially evolves in a very conservative fashion. This conservatism was the double-edged sword which authority faced when formalising worship. It was extremely difficult to establish a new religion and to maintain its forms while keeping to the hallowed traditions of the ancient ways of worship. If all the old stuff was swept aside, two results were probable; the first being that there might be no customers, and the second that there would be no magical insurance against mistakes—a delicate problem, which was never properly solved.

The documentary evidence within the Church, and the stylistic evolution of the chant from the vocalising of the people, is clear. The important implications in Chambers' work have been carefully under-stated, or easily passed over. The first omission is that of the *entire religious music* of the ancient world. Patristic evidence for the adaptation of the peasants' tuneful and joyous music to Christian worship seems almost too good to be true. All that was needed, apparently, was to add the correct words from the Psalter! This creative use of spontaneous music for worship, correctly channelled by the best texts, leaves a suspicious gap. Did the pagan priests and worshippers not use words and music? We know that they did, and that in Britain at any rate a strict mnemonic training was necessary for the priesthood.

There is a well-known controversy over which modes were con-sidered best for devotional use. This stems from two sources, the first being that the congregation were rumoured to sing unsuitable words to the airs that they already knew when these melodies were used in church. The second was connected with science of music and human reaction, as set out in various early works such as Plato's *Republic*, Aristotles' *Politics*, Augustine's *Confessions* and Boethius' *De Musica*.

It was usually assumed that the peasants were singing dirty songs to the adapted airs, as these were the kind of words that they would know best . . . and that we still encounter today occasionally, in movements such as the Salvation Army which set hymns to common tunes at their own risk.

The banished 'modus lascivus' of medieval music was the major scale, a favourite medium for bawdy songs even today. The early Christian problem was more likely to have been a direct confrontation between the liturgical material introduced, and that already in use. Knowing the incredibly conservative nature of common people's songs and music, we can assume that the congregations were using in worship words and music to which they were accustomed (such as the Dilly

Song). In many cases the actual church building was merely a new addition to an already hallowed temple-site and, as St Augustine informs us, the priests had only recently ceased to be flamens or druids. The mass of ordinary folk were not only accustomed to the formal paganism of whatever indigenous cult they followed, but would also have been familiar with a large body of ritual and superstition stemming from even earlier forms of worship. Any tradition is found to retain such forms at any time in its life history. It is not surprising, therefore, that the new religion was grafted on to old roots.

The most common pattern of primitive group-expression evolves into that of leader and chorus. This has the effect of continual rhythm and hypnotic magical reiteration, and is an easy form to learn and participate in. *The Cutty Wren*, *Down in yon Forest*, the 'Padstow May Song' and many other folksongs take this form, which has a close connection with group expression, even in basically narrative ballads. One most interesting and often-quoted example of this ancient form, once suppressed as being heretical, is *The Hymn of Jesus*. This Gnostic chant is made up of leading lines and chorus-responses linked to dancing, as in a large number of surviving folk-rites. The use of AMEN is an hypnotic group-response and a word of power, not a polite affirmation conclusion as it is today.

As has been frequently observed, many ballads within our folk-tradition may have had dance associated with them. If they imply ritual meaning the refrain-line may be suggestive of mimetic action. The use of dancing and singing together as acts of worship was discouraged by Christian authority and virtually suppressed, save for a few exceptions confined to those saints who had replaced earlier deities, on whose days the people danced.

This suppression was not simply due to the pagan origin of such modes of worship, but had a more subtle and very sound magical reason behind it. The ritual and folksongs collected in the twentieth century retain pagan symbolism, but despite their astonishing tenacity of survival, they have lost a most important aspect of pagan worship. This was the very significant and essential stage of orgiastic worship, the phase of Inspiration.

A vital part of free chanting, jubilation or ululation, has been conveniently forgotten, or deliberately concealed. This is the apparently inspired free singing of wordless music-noises occasionally accompanied by 'speaking in tongues'. The process is well known to anthropologists as a primitive ritual phase, and is still carried out by minor sects today such as Pentecostals, Voodoo worshippers and Charismatic Christians. The practice is best observed in tribal rituals, though in essence there is no difference between its occurrence in a jungle environment or in a sophisticated city-setting. In either case it is the direct effect of an induced trance or abnormal state, where chosen individuals seem to become possessed by gods, demons or spirits, and may writhe and make apparently meaningful utterances. The most famous example of this, of course, is the record in the New Testament. This incident (Acts 2.1) caused the early church to suppress the practice in general worship, as it was considered that the line of Apostolic succession should be contained within a select hierarchy, and not be open to challenge or argument.

Far from being a unique event, as we are led to believe, the phenomenon of inspiration was common in the ancient world, for most ritual practices were designed to lead to precisely that end. There was a definite phase of this character in the Western pagan rites, and this magical occurrence was the 'secret' reason why authority was very strict upon official texts. The practice was indulged by many early Christian sects (though later suppressed); yet it is not mentioned in Chambers' work, as it would have been considered heretical.

If we consider the general structure of the Divine King and sacrificial system of worship, we can readily understand the Christian prohibition of the 'inspiration phase', and we may then see how it is relevant to our study of folksong. After the customary building up of ritual mood by repetitive chanting and dancing, the celebrants arrived at a moment of climax which took various forms. The most common for the mass of people was the group-orgy, but occasionally a select group or chosen individual reverted to prophetic utterances while in a dis-associated state of awareness. Originally this represented the contact between seeress and the spirit of the sacrificed Victim. As these heretical practices were known to have been carried out by early Christians at their love-feasts, with claim to direct contact between Earth and Heaven, we can understand why such methods were frowned upon.

The Hymn of Jesus (see Song Appendix) is undoubtedly a ritual of this sort as, in a more corrupt form, are several folk-ballads and songs. *Down in Yon Forest*, for example, has all the elements of a ritual, with antiphonal structure, repetition, and a visual and symbolic religious climax.

Ralph Vaughan Williams (*Some tentative ideas on the origins of music*) observed an open-air preacher gradually break into a chant from inspired speech, and points out that the resultant notes were those that form the basic pattern of several British ritual songs, and of a body of folksongs in general. The melody of *Down in Yon Forest* harmonises well with that of *The Cutty Wren*, in the version given here, while one of the melodies of a Wren song from Pembrokeshire is identical to the 'Saint George' dirge of the Padstow May Song. It has been suggested that certain rituals throughout Britain—especially May songs—have a common melodic basis. The situation is actually more complex than such a theory implies, and to suggest that there is a basic melody, and that 'almost every known English May song is a variant of this tune' (Reg Hall and Mervyn Plunkett in the magazine *Ethnic*) is to carry a generalisation far too far: caution should be applied to such comparisons.

When we consider that the mock Geordie song *Cushie Butterfield* also shares a melody with Padstow's Saint George dirge, we can see why such caution is necessary. No-one would suggest *that* song was part of a pagan ritual system.

There are definite similarities between the Padstow Song (see Appendix), the *Hal an Tow* and the Helston Furry Dance, but there is no suggestion in the remains of our ritual music that there was a national liturgy, nor do we have evidence of a chant-school that used specific form for its ritual music. Apart from musical considerations, the historical perspective is so wide and covers such a large number of cultures and influences that we cannot draw broad conclusions from evidence that is not susceptible to historical analysis.

The strata of folksong are too intermixed for accurate judgement. This can be seen by the fact that there is very little evidence for an overall Christian liturgy or religion to be adduced from folk-sources, yet we know that such a religion has been in existence for centuries, with several well-established liturgies.

Pagan worship was not standardised in the same way as Christian worship, but consisted of a mixture of cults and rituals derived from various racial groups, and often strictly confined to certain geographical sites. It is likely that at certain times there were ascendant overall cults or central authorities, such as the political Druids who gave the Romans so much trouble. Such a relatively free system of worship would generate common elements in symbolism, as all were subject to the all-powerful curse or blessing of the Great Mother. It seems unlikely that musical forms would have been fixed nationally by decree, as these are the result of a later and different kind of culture. Folk-music breeds similar variants through a common mentality and shared experience of environment, and so would the religious musics of Western culture have grown up in a similar pattern. This music was worked up into a finely developed art and science by certain techniques of oral communication practised by the priesthood.

Musical forms such as leader and response, overall choruses and inspired solo passages, and certain shapes of melodic phrasing, are naturally common to the British people. Excluding the lost inspirationa element, this situation survived until quite recently in folk-music.

Perhaps the inspirational aspect was retained in the playing of instrumental music, which was not as vigorous a tradition in England as in Ireland, Scotland and Wales, but it certainly was not present in folk-songs. It is a common story that fiddle- and pipe-players get their music from the Fairies, or from the Devil, and that inspired improvisations were the work of the Fiend acting through the hands of the player. This concept persisted well into the nineteenth century, in the fables about the maestro Pagannini and in the dream-story behind Tartini's 'Devil's Trill'. The concept may still be found in the guise of odd people who believe that the spirits of dead composers inspire them to play or write music. Again, Blues players in the United States were supposed to meet the Devil at a crossroads, where he cut their nails down, and then swapped guitars with them.

These curious superstitions are usually found to apply to certain forms of erotic and frenzied music, and are occasionally linked with a popular legend about standing stones. The story is that when some abandoned sinners were dancing on the Sabbath the music of the fiddler or piper grew faster and faster, and wilder and wilder, until the dancers were turned to stone. The musician was in fact the Devil (*Deo Falsus*) in disguise. The legend has several levels of meaning, combining a childish explanation of the ancient sites of worship with a deeper memory of the rites that were carried out within them. Any inspired work is usually regarded in a primitive culture as being the result of traffic with spirits. Even today artists are treated with reverence and laden with gifts, and are the rare sources of obvious divinity recognisable in our culture, which is devoid of organic religion.

The origin of this respect for musicians and other creators is not simply appreciation for their work, but stems from the awe of the priest, priestess or shaman, thus relating the creative process to communication with the Other-world. Such Fairy-inspired music as that of the pipers and fiddlers was obviously the work of anti-Christian demons, and had to be banned and ridiculed by the Church. This is the more significant reason for the suppression of such music than the customary moral censure on sexual grounds that underlines the story of the wicked dancers, though they do, of course, reflect the fertility rites which were the central public contribution of the Old Religion.

After all is said, played, and done, we do not really know from where our music comes. Make your own choice—gods, demons, angels, fairies, or the racial or individual unconscious are simply different terms for the unknown mystery of artistic creation. Rationalising the terminology of such an act does not in any way explain the act itself.

The continuity of certain shapes within folk-music suggests that ritual material in particular inspires and is suggested by specific melodic

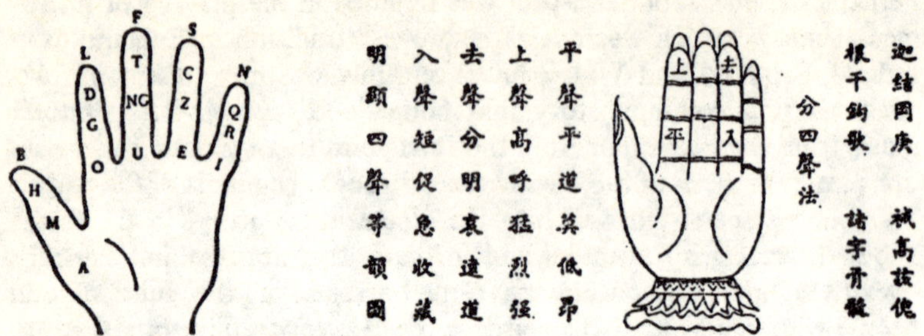

Mnemonic hands, common to both eastern and western systems
of symbolism, and still in use today in 'deaf-and-dumb' language
(drawings copied from Robert Graves and Hazedel-Levis)

phrases. The early notations of plainsong were 'shape notes' indicated by the hand (no-one is sure how), and there may be a connection between this chironomic system and the earlier Ogham alphabets of the Druids. If the division of the hand, or any other ground-base for the mnemonic oral work, had a symbolic meaning as in Ogham, Chinese music notation, and in Western magical and occult theory, then there is a common language of symbolism for ritual musics such as folk- and plain-song. The key to these has been lost or hidden. As this system was annexed for Christian use, we have another typical example of the key for old Mysteries being adapted to the benefit of newer cults, a constant religious and historical process.

The argument really centres upon the inexplicable fact that music is known to exalt or degrade human consciousness. If there is a body of knowledge that provides the means to uplift the soul in worship, then this is a valuable property—both spiritual, and ultimately, material. With centuries of research and usage from the sophisticated ancient religions in both East and West, music had developed as a divine science of psycho-sonics. It was therefore essential for any new faith or cult to make use of this science: if it were possible to control it entirely, then those in control would have the monopoly of spiritual power in worship. Hence the suppression of magical music and group ritualisation unless they were used by the Church. In later centuries this developed into disapproval of the sexual context of folk ceremonies, but these rituals held out stubbornly, despite every effort to expunge them from the popular imagination.

The entire question of witchcraft was basically political, as any religion closely tied to worldly government will naturally consider any older or rival faith to be a revolutionary threat.

The early missionaries, founders of the Celtic church reputed to be the true form of Christianity in the West, brought their revelation to a people with a highly developed group of religions; they may even have had a broad overall philosophy, as is suggested by the surviving evidence of Druid lore and ritual. As pagan symbolism was gradually adapted to the new faith, so was the music adapted as part of a catholic absorbtion and regeneration.

There are certain problems involved in the interpretation of early plainsong notation and technique. These could have their solution in the Druid or 'bardic' sources from which the chant must have been derived. If plainsong had really been *invented* at a certain point in time, as has been argued, it should not be shrouded in obscurity but would surely have been proclaimed as a divine asset. It should be better documented and more easily interpreted. The main modifications of plainsong that we know were not musical, but textual. Even the Gregorian modal definitions were imposed upon an already existing chant system.

It has been suggested that Ogham spelt out on the fingers of the hand, rather than the form in which it was cut into stones and sticks, was a secret code system. It is more likely that it was a non-verbal communication-process for use in ritual or musical situations where spoken instructions would have been unsuitable, and might spoil effect or concentration. This is still a practice used by ritualists of various sorts today, where mime or hand-motions, or soft hand-claps or body-movements are more effective than verbal directives. Hand-indications are used in various oriental musics which rely upon an oral and chironomic system for involved types of notation. Hand-movements and finger joints are used to indicate specific phrases and pitches rather than individual notes, as is the convention with written music.

Saint Augustine tells us how the Druid flamens became priests, and they would surely have contributed their knowledge and experience of Other-world techniques to the new cult. No expert who moves from job to job abandons his expertise when he leaves the old firm, else why would anyone re-employ him? The mysterious plainsong followed directly from pagan chant, such as is commonly developed within a true oral tradition where there is no general level of literacy.

The whole concept of modes in folk- and plain-song may be clarified by a simple understanding of the broad basis of early philosophical and religious thought, and its expression through music and song. Early alphabets, music, mathematics and images were all related as symbolic cycles. These systems were integrated in an attempt to render the Universe meaningful. They flow into one another, and are as interlinked as the seasons. A letter was a note, was a god or goddess, was a tree, was a star, was a season. All were cycles of the divine harmony of the music of the spheres. Patristic writings show that the ecclesiastical chant was drawn from existing practice, and subsequent measures of disguise tend to confirm this fact. The plainsong used adapted versions of the symbol-systems, represented in Britain by Ogham, as alphabetical and magical keys similar in style to astrology, the Tree of Life, and other structures of applied consciousness (see diagram of Tree of Life, etc.).

The actual phrases of music and patterns of notes may have been translatable originally as symbols, acting directly upon the sensibilities of the worshippers by choice of mode. This leads back finally to the ancient concept of the Dance of the Elements, and the Inneffable Holy Name. This concept survived at least as late as the Elizabethan era with the cryptographer Dr Dee, who claimed to have interpreted the Enochian language of Angels.

It is no wonder that there is little open evidence on the evolution of plainsong. It was not only a natural development of true 'jubilation', but was the key to aspects of the ancient Mysteries, now apparently lost.

Traditional music surviving today, in use or in collection, cannot be a direct link with such a system as has been inferred. It is, however, the organic basis from which such methods grow, and also the organic detritus to which they return when they break up and are forgotten. Again we find that folksong is not only the source of all music and poetry, but the end to which all such streams of creation come in time.*

---

*Those wishing to examine in greater detail the material of ancient music and its theories, should consult *The Greek Aulos* by Kathleen Schlesinger (Methuen). This very comprehensive and technical work proposes important theories based upon the laws of accoustics, which have direct bearing on the evolution of plainsong as a 'sacred science'.

The Survival of Pagan Cults

The subject of the survival of pagan worship as an established and secret set of cults, rather than as folk material, is complex. The historical picture is further complicated by the continual revival of cult-rituals from apparently respectable Christian sources. The whole issue has been grossly distorted by the assumption that formal Christianity is 'right' and belongs in context as an authoritative standard of judgement. Other cults therefore must, in the light of Christian history, be dismissed as false. One is reminded of the American devotee of an Eastern cult, whose guru told him not to go to a Benedictine Abbey 'as those places are full of evil spirits'.

Pagan worship survived in two ways. The first is in the form of any sort of intellectually based and formally maintained religion. The second is that of spontaneous and unconscious recurrence of certain kinds of worship and ritual activity, given form by old traditions of uncertain origin. To suggest that 'witchcraft' was the only religious descendent from ancient times is hardly sensible. There was undoubtedly a mainstream of pagan practice, which we can still recognise today, but it manifested itself through numerous sources, including both intentional cults and folk survivals.

The general assumption of the purity of Christian ritual and doctrine makes it difficult to remember that this particular cult achieved political ascendancy by absorbing and regenerating its predecessors. This does not preclude 'faith' or 'revelation', or deny any individual his or her personal religious beliefs. It is merely a statement of the natural growth of any and every cult to a position of supremacy, from which it becomes rapidly corrupt and decays. Later it may reform through smaller groups or sects, often gaining vitality by the way. This process had occurred within the Roman Empire when Christianity began to spread, and no doubt occurred earlier among the Druid hegemony of the Celtic realms. Folk-singers, still preserving certain ritual songs in the present century, went to Church and Chapel. There is no problem or contradiction in this—one was a formal religion established by state and social pressure, indoctrination and upbringing, a conventional form of recognised worship; the other a natural expression of life-forces. By the early nineteen-hundreds, the time had long passed when other cults were a threat to the new religion, which had begun its decline at least 200 years previously, despite all efforts at self-salvation.

It is clear that local cults of animal worship, crop- and weather-magic, and general healing were common well into the eighteenth century, despite all forms of repression. This contributes to the general conclusion that Britain was never a 'Christian' country. No country or race is ever wholly of one faith or religion (see for example evidence given by Margaret Murray, Lewis Spence, Frazer, Graves, Hargrave

Jennings, etc.). It seems unlikely that most of the folksongs of magic survived due to deliberate or secret ritual. They were part of the every-day life of the people who sang them, and not secret at all. The sus-picion and concealment that surrounds folksong and ritual is part of the incredible conservatism of any oral tradition, not due to motives of secrecy. People from outside one's immediate locality are still known as 'furriners' in parts of the West of England, and although their money is welcome, they are not desired to live in country areas, but merely to spend and pass through. Such hostility may be gradually disappearing, but suspicion of the stranger has deep roots which will rapidly reflower in a rural or closed community.

The Padstow May Ceremony is not thought of as being religious by the local people, yet it is surrounded by religious and ritualised be-haviour. Hostility has revived in recent years (1975–6) due to the bad manners of tourists who will not allow the local people room to dance. No-one would suggest that this ceremony, with an almost unbroken tradition, was actively anti-Christian, or that it was ever part of an underground religious movement. Yet it contains more of the real old religions, despite its open performance, than any of the suburban cults for housewives that have mushroomed since the repeal of the Witchcraft Act.

It is possible that in the not-too-distant past folk rituals such as the drink and dance orgies, dating back to pagan rites, may have helped to preserve and also regenerate certain songs and ballads which have magical themes. Many ballads are surely reinterpretations of myths, and a folk-ceremony is an intermediate step between ancient ritual and consciously revived drug- and drink-taking connected with ceremonial working as practised by witches.

If the music described at the many well documented witch-trials was folk-music—and it could hardly have been anything else—then we can be sure that the ancient forms of antiphonal chanting and linked dancing were used in these rites. The fact that we find a song such as *Down in Yon Forest* within the tradition does not suggest that there was a secret Grail-cult among the country people, who had probably never heard of the Romances. Some British folk were aware of Arthur and his prophesied return, but from a different and much older Celtic source than that of the refined Grail legends. The existence of ritual-songs shows us something far more wonderful than the possibility of secret cults, something far more magical. The survival of pagan images among the songs of the country-people, and in their annual and seasonal ceremonies, shows a constant tradition of magical relationship to Life. Natural survival of material of this sort need not imply revolution-ary secret orders, but is a true re-emergence of therapeutic and essential images in action.

It is this expressive and therapeutic element that helped to create folk-music and ritual in the prehistoric past, and which today causes people to return to such music for their delight. The joy and satisfaction of singing a magical song or dancing a ritual-dance is no mere fantasy. The value of this kind of activity is immense, and as our forefathers might have said, joins us to the spirits of our ancestors.

Certain traces of a hereditary priesthood may be found within our tradition, especially where the songs are part of a folk-ceremony. Song-collectors noticed that certain families were considered to be *the* singers, and to have rights to a certain song or songs, which no one else would sing, even if they did know it. The ritual honour of dancing at Padstow is supposed to be confined to descendants of Mayors of the town, a typical rationalisation, but it is definitely confined to certain families, and the singing is always led by women.

The right to sing certain songs may be a survival of the earlier cultures where there was no separation between music, song, worship and ritual invocation. The prowess of Druid bards has already been mentioned, and it seems likely that their chanting was adopted by the Church and passed into the broader stream of the native culture. The inhibitions against singing another person's song, especially if he or she was *the* singer as was often the case, is a conservative survival of the reluctance to encroach upon the magical territory of the medicine man, priest or shaman. It may be that at an earlier date these families of singers, players and dancers held a position in the rural community connected with medicine and weather or wisdom lore, but there is no suggestion that they were ever part of organised secret cults.

Group ceremonies such as the Rites of May are obviously similar to those denounced as 'devil worship. It is likely that the much commercialised 'witches' spontaneously revived their religion again and again, rather than kept it in a conscious state of preservation. The earlier centuries of Christian pagan conflict obviously did cause organised worship to go underground, often literally. The folk-memory does not retain conscious ritualism, or intellectualised secrecy, but works as in a dream. In this way, although words may be lost or confused, despite a tough oral memory, the spirit of the nature rites is still present. Whereas ritual itself may degenerate until the meaning is lost, the images of the gods and goddesses or powers involved live on in songs and acts that had no apparent surface religious elements.

When St Augustine, in the Fourth Century A.D., railed against 'that most filthy habit of dressing up as horse or stag', and when the Puritans centuries later preached against the licentious behaviour of the people, they were describing the same rituals, separated by over 1000 years. When certain 'respectable' people in Cornwall attempted to ban Maying in the nineteenth century, or at least substitute harmless pastimes in its stead, they were also reacting against those same rituals. The magical ballads have escaped close attention because of their unobtrusive nature, but one sometimes wonders if television and pop-culture have at last succeeded in destroying what the powers of Christianity could never touch.

The images of the mass media are fundamentally expressions of the gods and goddesses. Any witness to a mass concert of popular music will realise the close similarity to orgiastic worship as described classically—the pounding rhythms, the sexual music, the use of drugs, the mass release of inhibitions through submersion in a group-mind are all typical aspects. Dominating the entire pattern are the cult figures of the artists, performing well-rehearsed sounds and motions to excite and command the energies of their devotees. This is the giant-scale contemporary version of the ritual behaviour of the ancient world, where priests and priestesses utilised the energies of the people to bring the community closer to the Mother Goddess or to her Son. Today those energies are unscrupulously drained away for the purposes of profit, with no return or sense of life-participation being offered. The ritual-dramas of official and unofficial religions use exactly the same elements, though the tradition of orgiastic ceremony has been eliminated from Christian practice.

Under the sublimating and auto-erotic influence of television and pop-culture sales pressure, folksongs do not flourish. In those areas of the West Country where the songs examined in this book were collected the only folksong likely to be heard today would be on record or radio or sung by local 'folk' enthusiasts in the pub. Yet the attraction of the music is not lost. Nor is the memory of it. Only five years ago an elderly lady in North Devon heard the author playing a folk-dance tune. She asked what it was, and on being told, replied, 'Oh . . . so *that's* folk music! We used to dance to those tunes years ago when I was a girl. . . . I didn't think *that* was folk music!' Obviously she had been conditioned to think that folk-music was the commercial product offered by record companies, which still has a stranglehold on the popular revival of traditional music and song. No-one would suggest that when she and her friends were dancing over half-a-century previously they were maintaining an old religion, but they were undoubtedly using music that was originally ritualistic.

There is no separation between magical and non-magical activity, the difference being in the quality and direction of motive, rather than in the expression itself. This is why religious material survives within the folk tradition without being maintained by cult-worship. In fact, cult-worship tends to degenerate more rapidly than folk memory or spontaneous ritual.

111

The issue of the 'evil' nature of folk-rites is designed to obscure and destroy such forms of worship. Certainly, over the centuries many practices degenerated into pointless human and animal sacrifice—as did loving kindness and the imitation of Christ turn into persecution and mass-murder. The evil lies in human weakness, and not necessarily in the inherent qualities of any particular cult. As far as folk-material is concerned the ritual elements and symbols are neutral, and may be adapted for beneficial or destructive results. Puritan attitudes to folk-song still persisted into the twentieth century, and members of chapel-sects believed that the music that was sung in the pub or at small social gatherings was sinful.

This included the old songs and ballads, as well as semi-literary paeans to the demon drink, usually composed by country vicars.

Strictly speaking, such a bigotted attitude is correct. Opposing cults are evil in each others' eyes, and it is amusing to find a folk-memory of religious conflict through the puritan stream of inheritance, when the original indoctrination was set up by the Catholic Church. This sin *motif* is still in action, long after the original battle has become irrelevant through the development of new attitudes to life.

The pagan quality of folksong is no longer manifested in the sense, but in the imagery. Many folk-ballads were originally ritualistic, especially the group-workings linked to dance and mime. If we study the possibility of folksong in pagan worship, then many folksongs are found to be 'educational'. An oral tradition does not necessarily expect its members to know the meaning of the material . . . the prime value lies in correct reproduction. It is customary in active traditions which use ritual and initiation techniques to be given lines or riddles that are revealed or explained only gradually. Sometimes this process extends over a number of years, long after the original lines were first learned. Some of our folksongs contain such initiatory and magical keys, such as the *Dilly Song*. We can easily appreciate their religious origin by the fact that a Christian interpretation has been forced upon them, though with difficulty. A similar occurrence has happened to *Down in Yon Forest*, already quoted, which is not only an invocation, but also a theophany.

Pagan elements are found in many such songs and early carols, but in folk-carols rather than composed pieces. To unravel the symbolism of *The Leaves of Life*, an apparently Christian Carol, or *The Bitter Withy* or the *Cherry Tree Carol* is to be left with the strands of a pagan weaving. (See Song Appendix, p. 121.)

Some of these songs could be the oral remnants of religious instruction, and this may suggest an underground stream of survival. There is doubt over the success of the suppression of the old religions, and we do not know if such suppression was ever successful to any great degree. The incredible tenacity of the oral tradition and its regenerative power stemming from fertility urges suggest that an underground tradition was not really necessary. At an early transitional period, country people merely continued to sing and behave as they had always done towards the old gods; the new Divine Son was merely another part of a growing pattern. Orgiastic worship, which later became the witch-'cult', had been officially banned by the Roman Empire long before Christianity appeared. Actual witchcraft is the heir of a very old religion indeed, allied to chthonic powers and a Mother Goddess.

When the folk witches met in secret, they used drugs to recover the images of the old faith, through a trance type of process in which such images will occur. The problem of accurate definition still remains to be solved, as all pagan rituals were eventually classed as 'witchcraft', whereas the true cult was influenced but not absorbed by Celtic culture, and was an infernal religion.

The argument rests upon the *conscious* quality of worship. If a ritual is deliberately carried out with the intention of worshipping or invoking god or goddess X or Y, then it is part of a religion, and has some philosophy behind it. If, however, this conscious avowal is not present we have a folk ceremony, open to any form of rationalisation put upon it by the celebrants. The magical-religious symbols are kept alive in an oral tradition through their unconscious appeal. If you ask a folk ritualist why he or she performs a certain action, or why it is done with a certain song, the reply is 'because it has to be done' or 'because it has always been done this way'.

Where from Here?

THE NEW SAINT GEORGE
(a contemporary popular song by Richard Thompson.)

The time has come for action, so leave your satisfaction,
Can't you hear St George's tune?
St George's tune is calling you on!
The earth she was your mother, so fight for one another,
And leave the factory, leave the forge,
And dance to the new St George.

Don't believe pretenders, who say they will defend us,
While they flash their teeth and wave,
The other hand is being paid—
They choke the air and bleed us, those noble men who lead us,
So leave the factory, leave the forge,
And dance to the new St George.

The fish and fowl are ailing, the farmer's life is failing,
Where are all the backroom boys?
The backroom boys can't save us now!
We're poisoned by the greedy, who plunder from the needy,
So leave the factory, leave the forge,
And dance to the new St George.

This is a modern popular song. It is a good example of the increasing awareness that our basic roots of life are threatened, and it instinctively draws upon the right hero-image, the Saviour of Britain, descendant of Bran and Arthur, heir of Beli and of Archangel Michael. On a less obvious level, a great interest in real folk-music and song, dance and lore, is slowly developing out of the commercial revival of folksong.

This growing interest is a direct response to the conditioning of mass media and commercial music, which has now reached almost saturation-point. People begin to turn instinctively to their racial roots for both entertainment and inspiration when they realise that the fruits of accepted society are surely rotten. This reversion is at first an intellectual process, because the true folk tradition is dead, but it derives from an intuitive call from our musical and poetical racial home. There dwell the deities of our ancestors, close to the energy of life that causes us to make songs, music, images and dreams. Today this energy is being deliberately channelled into the most useless patterns for monetary gain, and people are beginning to seek better outlets and to search for genuine responses not prompted by greed.

Our present 'folk revival' is not very creative. It functions on a level of entertainment, drawing material loosely from traditional sources as found in print or on a few rare recordings. It has developed a commercial style and flavour of its own, quite far removed from the tradition that inspired it, and hardly representative of true racial music. This process of experiment and development is not necessarily bad, nor is it likely to damage the spirit of our racial imagery and symbolism. In course of time unsuitable material is easily forgotten, and the pseudo-folk songs that have appeared in the past few years will disappear just as easily, leaving no mark upon whatever folk tradition does survive.

This brings us to the question—do we have a tradition of any sort left? Do we have anything to hand on to the future other than a large collection of dull books and commercial recordings? More disturbing is the question—is there no future at all for folk-music, is it being erased from the mass mind by generations of television, anti-education, commercial music and advertising psychology?

In point of fact we do not know where we are going from here. Our true tradition may spring up again in new forms, or it may yet be suppressed beyond all recovery. It would be an inestimable loss if the vital and powerful images of our native mythology were lost beyond recall, or at best, reduced to commercial slave status. These forms of music and imagery are not merely exciting and beautiful, they are essential for our very life, for our growth and evolution. Mention has already been made of the therapeutic value of such material today, for these symbols are the common path to mental and emotional development. They hold the only true experience of our entire people, and are clear signposts upon the road to increased awareness. At certain times, specific images and concepts have developed into formal religions which rise, thrive and decay. The tradition itself is not religious, but transcends religious expression and flows beneath it. A tradition leads where it will, recreating itself along the way.

But if the tradition is deliberately denied, as at the present time, our energies have no broad stream in which to flow, and are channelled into the useless backwaters of consumer orientation. The strong flow of a tradition is the basis from which individual effort arises and from which great developments take place. The redundant state of serious music, and the blatant corruption of popular music, are typical of forms of creation that have become isolated from their native tradition. Intellectual arrogance begins the process of isolation, which is completed by intentional commercialism. It is vitally necessary to shatter the idol-images of self-devouring art and soul-destroying pop cults.

A tradition makes or unmakes itself, and is influenced by factors difficult to observe. If our music, poetry and inner images are to revive, they will only do so within the consciousness of large numbers of people, quite spontaneously. Present efforts at conservation offer a record of the valuable material that we have inherited from a way of life now lost, and it is essential that this alternative be available for comparison with the false images that are continually projected by the media. But more is needed than mere collection and classification. The phase of collection has passed, as has the revival by classical composers. It is imperative that we recreate and express the spirit of our folk-consciousness and project it into the future by putting it to work in the present. Works of reference are, of course, of some value to this end, but only if they contribute to a living participation in the growth and rebirth of a noble tradition. Such work, like that of the well-meaning classical musicologists who ruined folksong for a generation or more by forcing it on to the school piano, can easily fail. In England we need only look at the official dance and song organisation to be reminded that the vision of Ralph Vaughan Williams, Cecil Sharp and of many other inspired workers has been degraded by lesser minds.

A moving incident is related of Sharp being seized by the woman singing to him, who with tears in her eyes said, 'Isn't it beautiful? Isn't it beautiful?' This ecstatic appreciation of natural music is hardly echoed by what is currently offered to the public as folksong and dance.

An interesting recent development in our sorry tale of folk revival is an increasing awareness of instrumental music, particularly from the Irish and Scots traditions. The main hope for an increased standard of performance seems to come from this broadly 'Celtic' revival, now that it is passing its commercial teething stage. Its value is in its purely melodic and 'modal' style, which gives a great boost to the representation of British songs and music. The limitation of folk-revivalists is that they have seldom achieved understanding of the true nature of their own music, but have allowed musical conditioning and modern harmonic tricks to influence their treatment of the material, both in thought and in performance. Even Cecil Sharp, who was well aware of the modal nature of folksongs, was quite unable to arrange the music according to its own laws. The increasing popularity of good 'Celtic' music helps to raise standards and to cause the public to demand more thoughtful instrumental treatment of the songs and music. The days of the rigid piano were closed by the unavoidable guitar, which has strummed and thrashed its way through folk-music—where it is as alien as the key-board—for three decades. Abuse of this sort does nothing for either the instrument or the music.

Recently people have begun to realise that there are other instruments better suited to their native music. Guitars are being put away and out come fiddles, flutes, concertinas, flageolets, harps, pipes—Highland, Lowland, Northumbrian and Uilleann—drums of all shapes and sizes, citterns, plucked and hammered dulcimers and plucked and bowed psalteries. This exciting revival of folk-instruments produces a glorious range of tones and sounds (not all perfect). Already the Uilleann pipes and the Celtic Harp are competing on the international pop-concert stage with the tyrannical mountains of electronics used to hide the inadequacies of incompetent musicians.

If enough good folk-music and song is well performed, and can be communicated to a large number of people through the mass-media in addition to private gatherings, clubs and festivals, then we need have less concern for our future. If the music is suppressed in favour of commercial products that have no depth other than that of the publishers' purse, we cannot expect anything other than the continuing fall in standards that most people are conditioned to accept. But if we take care of public representation of folk-material, then the future rebirth of a tradition will surely take care of itself.

The message of the native tradition, common to us all, is that death is followed by rebirth in one world or another, in one way or another. This in itself should give us hope. All those who believe in the beauty and value of the native tradition in any of its forms, British or American, should work in every possible way to ensure that its rebirth is not moulded in any way by contemporary mind-inhibiting techniques, but is allowed to flower freely out of its true roots, and to grow as it wills in the human awareness.

> Oh the Lily and the gentle Rose
> The Rose upon the Thorn,
> Amen, Dear Lord, and Charity—
> Is the ending of my song.

Appendix of Songs

DOWN IN YON FOREST

(or *Lullay*, the 'Corpus Christi' carol)

Variants of this well known carol give a clear progression of visual symbols. This process, which can be followed in either of the versions quoted here, though both may be incomplete, is common to both early Mystery and meditation techniques, and to modern psycho-therapy. The images used, of waste land, orchard, forest, bower, hall, blood and wounded man, all stem from a Celtic theme, which later developed into the story of the Holy Grail. They are not merely historical remnants, but are the images which arise in our minds, representing certain individual and generally human states of being.

The interesting appearance of the maiden sitting upon the stone (which in some verses has 'Corpus Christi' written upon it) should remind us immediately of another maiden in balladry. The curious lady in Giles Collins, also connected with the death of a hero, washed a marble stone in the stream, and sewed a silver seam. Such images identify themselves by their functions, and often occur in songs which are not outwardly related. Such clues mark a song not only as being ritual or magical, but also with a particular cult and culture. This does not suggest that the song concerned originated in the religion that is linked with it by such symbols, but shows that the ballad absorbed such material in the past, and enabled it to survive.

The lady with the silver thread is the ancient Goddess, weaving the thread of Life, by which the victim's soul was bound up in one direction to his body, and in the other to his stellar destiny. The use of the stone image is clearly stated in the Christian adaptation. We know that stones were never identified in the Mass with the body of Christ, but we also know that ancient stones were used in worship, often with a sacrificial function. It was a common primitive belief that a man's soul was tied up with his special stone. Such stones were given or passed on to an individual upon his initiation into manhood, and the use of stone circles in our native worship was possibly connected with this universal practice.

DOWN IN YON FOREST

Down in yon forest there stands a hall,
The Bells of Paradise I heard them ring,
Is covered all over with purple and pall,
And I love my lord Jesus above anything.

And all in that Hall there stands a bed,
Is covered all over in scarlet and red

And all on that bed there lies a knight
Whose wounds do bleed with main and might

And all from his wounds there runs a flood,
The one half is water the other half blood.

And at the beds foot there lies a hound
A licking the blood as it daily runs down

And all at the beds head there flowers a thorn
That never so blossomed since Adam was born.

*   *   *

Lullay lullay lullay lullay,
The falcon hath borne my maker away.

She bore him up and she bore him down
She bore him into an orchard brown.

The heron flew east and the heron flew west
She flew over a fair forest.

And there she spied an orchard fair
Wherein grew the apple and pear

And in that orchard standeth a hall
Was hanged down with purple and pall

And in that hall there standeth a bower
Was covered all over with lily flowers

And in that bower there standeth a bed
Is covered o'er with gold so red

And in that bed there lieth a knight
Whose wounds do bleed with main and might

And under the bed there runneth a flood
The one half water and the other half blood

By that bed there lieth a stone
With a leal maiden sitting thereon

With silver needle and golden thread
A stemming the wounds that daily do bleed.

(*see* 'Giles Collins')

THE LEAVES OF LIFE

All under the Leaves and the Leaves of Life,
I met with Virgins Seven,
One of them was Mary mild—
Our Lord's first Mother in Heaven.

O where are you going to, you seven pretty maids,
All under the leaves of light?
Oh we are going, Thomas they said,
Seeking for a friend of thine.

And they went down into yonder town
And sat in the Gallery,
And there they saw sweet Jesus Christ
Hanging from a big Yew Tree.

Oh do not weep for me Mother,
Oh do not for me grieve,
For I must suffer this, he said,
For Adam and for Eve.

Oh how can I my weeping cease,
My sorrows to forgo, when I see my own son die
And sons I have no more?

He's laid his head on his right shoulder,
And death soon drew him nigh,
May the Holy Ghost receive my soul,
Dear Mother now I die.

Oh the rose, the gentle rose,
The fennel it grows so strong,
Amen, dear Lord, to thy Charity,
Is the ending of my song.

SEVEN WAS THE KEYS OF HEAVEN

(The Dilly Song)

(sung as part of the Barton Hill Mummers' Play, Bristol)

What shall I sing?
Sing all over twelve.
What was twelve?
Twelve was the keys of Hell
Eleven was the Crown of Heaven,
Ten was a golden Pen,
Nine was a glass of wine
Eight was a landscape
Seven was the keys of Heaven
Six was a Crucifix
Five was a man alive
Four was a lady's birth
Three was eternity
Two was a jury
One was God the righteous man
Who sent our souls to rest, Amen.

THE HYMN OF JESUS

(based upon GRS Meads' translation from THE LEUCIAN ACTS)

Glory to Thee, Father, (and we going round in a ring answered to Him)
*   AMEN.*
Glory to The, Logos—Amen
Glory to thee, Charis—Amen
Glory to thee Spirit—Amen
Glory to thee Holy One—Amen
Glory to thy Glory—Amen

We praise Thee, Oh Father
We give thanks to Thee oh Light
In whom Darkness dwells not
Amen.

I would be saved and I would save—Amen
I would be loosed and I would loose—Amen
I would be wounded and I would wound—Amen
I would be consumed for love and I would consume—Amen
I would beget and I would be begotten—Amen
I would eat and I would be eaten—Amen
I would hear and I would be heard—Amen
I would wash and I would be washed—Amen
I would pipe, dance ye all—Amen
I would dirge, lament ye all—Amen
The Eight sounds with us—Amen
The Twelve lead the Dance—Amen
All dance who dance in nature—Amen
Who danceth not knows not what cometh—Amen
I would flee and I would stay—Amen
I would adorn and I would be adorned—Amen
I would be at-oned, and I would at-one—Amen
I have no dwelling and I have dwellings—Amen
I have no place and I have places—Amen
I have no temple and I have temples—Amen
I am a lamp to thee who seest me—Amen
I am a mirror to thee who understands me—Amen
I am a door to thee who knockest at me—Amen
I am a way to thee, a wayfarer—Amen

(a section is omitted here, and the verses conclude as follows)

But as for me, if thou wouldst known what I was;
In a word I am the Word who did dance all things
and was not shamed at all.
'Twas I who leapt and danced.

But do thou understand all, and understanding say:
Glory to Thee, Father—Amen.

(*And having danced these things with us, Beloved, the Lord went forth. And
we, as though beside ourselves, or wakened out of deep sleep, fled each our
several ways.*)

GILES COLLINS

Giles Collins rode out on a May morning
When May was all in bloom
And there he espied, and there he espied a fair pretty maid,
She was washing of a marble stone.

She hooped and she hollered she highered her voice,
She held up her lily white hand,
Oh come hither to me, ah come hither to me,
Giles Collins she said,
And your life it will not last long.

He set his foot on the broadwater side,
And over the river jumped he,
And he caught her around, he caught her around the middle so small
And he kissed her three times three.

Giles Collins rode back to his father's own hall,
Oh mother come make up my bed,
And I will ask, and I will ask
My own sister dear,
For a knapkin to tie round my head.

And if I should chance to die this night,
As I suppose I shall,
Do you bury me neath, you bury me neath
That marble stone,
That stands by fair Elanor's hall.

Fair Elanor sat in her tower on high,
She was sewing a silver seam,
And there she espied, and there she espied
A coffin a coming,
It was the fairest that ever she'd seen.

And she said all unto her own servant maid,
Whose coffin is this so fine?
Oh indeed and it is, indeed and it is
Giles Collins that's coming,
And he once was a lover of thine.

O lay him down and lay him down,
And lay him down so fine,
And I will kiss, and I will kiss
Giles Collinses lips,
Oh for many times he kissed mine.

And you go upstairs and fetch of the sheet
That's woven with a silver twine,
And you wrap it around, you wrap it around (or hang it above)
Giles Collinses head,
Oh and tomorrow twill hang above mine.

The news it was carried to fair London town,
And written on London gate, that six pretty maids (× 2)
All died in one night, and it's all for Giles Collins sake.

In addition to the connection of the heroine of this ballad with various divine
images in other songs, the story given here, collected in both England and

in the U.S.A. in ballad form during the early part of the twentieth century, has a close link with Irish legend. The plot is almost identical to a tale told of the Daghdha (The Good God), one of the leaders of the Tuatha De Danann. He met with a woman on the ancient feast day of Samhain (November 1st), who was standing astride a river, washing. He made love to her, and she identified herself as being the Goddess of fate and slaughter (the Morrighan), who was believed to appear before a battle washing the bodies of those doomed to die. Curiously, the Daghdha was connected with the Cauldron, in various tales, and we find this Lady again in variants of the Corpus Christi carol, undoubtedly part of the 'Grail' mythology.

THE LAILLY WORM

My father he married the worst woman that ever your eyes did see,
And she was a witch of the vilest of kind, and a lady of high degree.

She turned me into the Lailly Worm, to coil all around the tree,
And she turned my sister Maisry to the Mackerel of the Sea.

And every night at evening time the Mackerel comes to me,
And she combs of my hair with a long silver comb and washes it in the sea.

And seven brave knights I have slain here, all underneath of the tree,
And even if you were my own father dear, the eighth one you should be.

So his father he sent for this lady so gay and all unto her he did say
'And what have you done with my young son, and sister Maisry?'

'Oh your son he has gone all to the king's court, earning his meat and fee,
And your daughter has gone all to the queen's court, a lady for to be.'

'You lie and you lie, you evil woman, so loud I hear you to lie,
For you turned my son to the Lailly Worm to coil around the tree
And you turned his sister Maisry to the Mackerel of the Sea.'

So the lady has taken a long silver wand and stroked it three times three,
And up and arose then the finest young knight that ever a son could be.

And the lady has taken a small silver horn and blown on it three times three,
And all of the fishes they came unto her but the Mackerel of the Sea.

And all of the fishes they came unto her but the Mackerel of the Sea,
'For you shaped me once in an unseemly shape and you never more will shape me.'

So the lord he has sent all to the greenwood for the whin and for the hawthorn,
And there he has taken that lady so gay, and there he did her burn . . .
And there he has taken that lady so gay, and there he did her burn.

LONG LANGKIN

Said my lord to my lady, as he mounted his horse,
Beware of Long Langkin that lives in the moss.

Said my lord to my lady as he rode away,
Beware of Long Langkin that lives in the hay.

Let the doors be all bolted and the windows all pinned
And leave not a hole for a mouse to creep in.

So he saddled and bridled and he rode away,
And he was in London ere the break of the day.

The doors were all bolted and the windows all pinned,
but for one little window where Long Langkin crept in.

Oh where's the lord of this house? said Long Langkin,
He's away in fair London, said the false nurse to him.

And where's the little son of the house? said Long Langkin,
He's asleep in his cradle, said the false nurse to him.

We'll prick him all over, we'll prick him with a pin,
And see if that'll bring his dear lady down to him.

So they pricked him all over, they pricked him with a pin,
And the nurse held a basin for the blood to run in.

Oh nurse how you slumber, oh nurse how you snore,
You leave my little son Johnson to cry and to roar.

Oh nurse how you slumber, oh nurse how you sleep,
You leave my little son Johnson to cry and to weep.

Oh I've tried him with an apple,
and I've tried him with a pear,
Come down my fair lady and rock him in your chair.

I've tried him with milk and I've tried him with pap
Come down my fair lady and rock him in your lap.

How can I come down in the dead of the night,
With no fire burning and no candlelight?

You have three silver mantles as bright as the sun
Come down my pretty lady all by the light of one.

My lady came down, and she thought it no harm,
And there stood the Langkin and caught her by the arm.

There's blood in the kitchen, there's blood in the hall,
And there's blood on the stairs where my lady did fall.

The maiden looked out from the turret so high
And she saw her master from London riding by.

Oh master oh master don't lay the blame on me
twas the false nurse and Langkin that murdered your lady.

THE BITTER WITHY

As it fell out on a high holiday
Small hail from the sky did fall,
Our Saviour asked his Mother dear,
If he could play at ball.

At ball at ball, my own dear son,
It's time that you were gone,
But don't let me hear of no mischief,
tonight when you gets home.

So its up the hill and down the hill
Our sweet young Saviour ran,
Until he spied three rich young lords
Was playing in the sun.

Good morning, good morning, good morning all cried he,
And which of you three rich young lords
Will play at ball with me?

Oh we're all lords and ladies sons,
Born in the highest hall,
And you are nothing but a poor Jews' child
And we won't play at ball.

So he built him a bridge of the beams of the sun,
And over the river ran he,
Those rich young lords followed after him,
And drowned was all three.

And up the hill and down the hill
Three rich young mothers ran,
saying Mary mild bring home your child,
For ours he's drowned each one.

So Mary mild brought home her child
And laid him across her knee
And with a bundle of withy twigs,
She gave him slashes three.

Oh bitter withy, ah bitter withy
You've made me for to smart,
And the withy shall be the very first tree
To perish at the heart.

THE PADSTOW MAY SONG

NIGHT SONG

Unite and unite and let us all unite
For summer is acome unto day
And whither we are going we will all unite
In the merry morning of May

*I warn you young men everyone
To go into the greenwood and fetch your May home*

*Arise up Mr . . . . and joy you betide
And bright is your bride that lies by your side.*

*Arise up Mrs . . . . and gold be your ring
And give to us a cup of ale the merrier we shall sing*

*Arise up Miss . . . . all in your gown of green
You are as fine a lady as wait upon the Queen.*

*Now fare you well, and we bid you all good cheer,
We call once more unto your house before another year.*

DAY SONG

*Unite and Unite and Let us All Unite,
For summer is acome unto Day
And Whither we are going we will all Unite
In the Merry Morning of May.*

*Arise up Mr . . . . I know you well and fine
You have a shilling in your purse and I wish it were in mine*

*All out of your beds
Your chamber shall be strewed with the white rose and the red.*

*Where are the young men that here now should dance
Some they are in England and some they are in France.*

*Where are the maidens that here now should sing
They are in the meadows the flowers gathering.*

*Arise up Mr . . . . with your sword by your side
Your steed is in the stable awaiting for to ride.*

*Arise up Miss . . . . and strew all your flowers
It is but a while ago since we have strewed ours.*

DIRGE

*Oh where is Saint George?
Oh where is he Oh?
He is out in his longboat
All on the salt sea Oh.*

*Up flies the kite
Down falls the lark Oh
Aunt Ursula Birdhood she had an old ewe,
And she died in her own park-O.*

*With the merry ring adieu the merry spring
How happy is the little bird that merrily doth sing*

The young men of Padstow they might if they would
They might have built a ship and guilded her with gold

The young women of Padstow they might if they would
They might have made a garland with the white rose and the red

Arise up Mr . . . . and reach me your hand
And you shall have a lively lass with a thousand pounds in hand

Arise up Miss . . . . all in your cloak of silk
And all your body underneath as white as any milk.

REPEAT DIRGE

Now fare you well and bid you all good cheer
We call no more unto your house until another year.

THOMAS THE RHYMOUR
(Child, vol. I)

1. *True Thomas lay oer yond grassy bank*
   And he beheld a ladie gay,
   A ladie that was brisk and bold,
   Come riding oer the fernie brae.

2. *Her skirt was of the grass-green silk,*
   Her mantel of the velvet fine,
   At ilka tett of her horse's mane
   Hung fifty silver bells and nine.

3. *True Thomas he took off his hat,*
   And bowed him low down till his knee:
   'All hail thou mighty Queen of Heaven!
   For your peer on earth I never did see.'

4. *'O no, O no, True Thomas,' she says,*
   'That name does not belong to me;
   I am but the queen of fair Elfland,
   And I'm come here for to visit thee . . .

5. *But ye maun go wi me now, Thomas,*
   True Thomas, ye maun go wi me,
   For ye maun serve me seven years,
   Thro weel or wae as may chance to be.'

6. *She turned about her milk-white steed,*
   And took True Thomas up behind,
   And aye whene'er her bridle rang,
   The steed flew swifter than the wind.

7. *For forty days and forty nights*
   He wade thro red blude to the knee,
   And he saw neither sun nor moon,
   But heard the roaring of the sea.

8. *O they rade on, and further on,*
   Until they came to a garden tree:
'Light down, light down, ye ladie free,
   Some of that fruit let me pull to thee.'

9. *'O no, O no, True Thomas,' she says*
   'That fruit maun not be touched by thee,
For a' the plagues that are in hell
   Light on the fruit of this countrie.

10. *'But I have a loaf here in my lap,*
    Likewise a bottle of claret wine,
And now ere we go farther on,
    We'll rest awhile, and ye may dine.'

11. *When he had eaten and drunk his fill,*
    'Lay down your head upon my knee,'
The lady sayd, 'ere we climb yon hill,
    And I will show you fairlies three.

12. *'O see not ye yon narrow road,*
    So thick beset wi thorns and briers?
That is the path of righteousness,
    Tho after it but few enquires.

13. *'And see not ye that bonny road,*
    Which winds about the fernie brae?
That is the road to fair Elfland,
    Whe(re) you and I this night maun gae.'

14. *'And see not ye that braid braid road*
    That lies across yon lillie leven?
That is the path of wickedness,
    Tho some call it the road to heaven.'

15. *'But Thomas, ye maun hold your tongue*
    Whatever you may hear or see,
For gin ae word you should chance to speak,
    You will ne'er get back to your ain countrie.'

16. *He has gotten a coat of the even cloth*
    And a pair of shoes of velvet green
And till seven years were past and gone
    True Thomas on earth was never seen.

SELECT BIBLIOGRAPHY

Introduction *and* The Tradition

FRAZER, J. G. *The Golden Bough* 1907–15
GRAVES, R. *The White Goddess* 1961
WIMBERLEY, L. C. *Folklore in English and Scottish Ballads* 1959
CHILD, F. J. *The English and Scottish Popular Ballads* 1882–98
ARMSTRONG, *Folklore of Birds*
SPENCE, L. *Mysteries of Britain* et al.
BARING-GOULD, S. & SHEPPARD, H. F. *Songs of the West* 1913
BROADWOOD, LUCY *English Traditional Songs and Carols* 1908
SHARP, C. J. *Folk Songs from Somerset* (5 vols) 1904–9
       English Folk Songs from the Southern Appalachians (2 vols) 1960
       English Folk Songs: some conclusions (4th ed.) 1965
WILLIAMS, R. V. & LLOYD, A. L. *The Penguin Book of English Folk Songs* 1959
MACCANA, P. *Celtic Mythology* 1975
ARMSTRONG, *The Wren*
JONES, G. & W. *The Mabinogion* 1950
ROSS, ANNE, *Pagan Celtic Britain* 1967

Who is Saint George?

BARING-GOULD, S. *Lives of the Saints*
BUTLER, *Lives of the Saints*
BUDGE, W., *Miracles and Martyrdom of St George of Cappadocia* 1888
HUTTON, W. H. *The English Saints* 1903
WILLIAMS, META, C. '*Whence came St George?*' in *Bulletin de la Société Royale
    d'Archæologie d'Alexandria*
RAWE, D. R. *Padstow's Obby Oss* 1971
ALFORD, VIOLET *Sword Dance and Drama* 1962 (and other works)
JENNINGS, H., *The Rosicrucians* 1887 (and other works)

The Keys of Heaven

GRAY, W. G. 'The Ladder of Lights' & 'Magical Ritual Methods', 1968–9
FORTUNE, D. *The Mystical Qabalah* 1935
MEAD, G. R. S. *The Hymn of Jesus* (translation & commentary), 1963
ANON. *The Work of the Chariot* (translations & commentary from the Hebrew),
    1971

Musical Considerations

CHAMBERS, G. B. *Folksong-Plainsong* (2nd ed.) 1972
BRONSON, B. H. *The Traditional Tunes for the Child Ballads*
LEVIS, J. HAZEDEL, *Chinese Musical Art*
BOETHIUS, *De Musica*

STEINER, R. *Eurythmy as Visible Speech*
         Eurythmy as Visible Song
WAGNER *A History of Plainchant*

The Survival of Pagan Cults

MURRAY, DR MARGARET *The God of the Witches*
                    The Divine King In England

FOLKSONG AND MUSIC ON RECORD

Folk-music and song on disc or tape may be divided into two main categories. The first is that of real folk material, recorded 'in the field' from a living oral tradition. The second, and much larger group of recordings, are of 'revival' material, an artistic and commercial repertoire broadly based upon folk styles. This area of music and song has had a rapid evolution, and now includes modern compositions with little or no identifiable traditional influence. Record companies tend to classify music as 'folk' in a very arbitrary manner, usually depending upon whether the instruments used are accoustic or electric. Hence a songwriter recording with an ordinary guitar may be listed as a 'folksinger', whereas one with an electric backing group is a 'pop' or 'rock' artist. The entire issue is very confused, and stems from a complete lack of awareness of the identity of traditional *style*.

Both field and revival recordings reveal interesting insights into the persistent reappearance of folk-music and poetry as both spontaneous and artistic utterances. A selection of recordings to illustrate the theories proposed in this book will contain examples of each type, especially as there are numerous revival recordings which demonstrate ballads and songs restored from print into living music.

The list is short, and the main qualification of its contents is not simply authenticity, but spirit. The suggested records should give a broad basis for developing a better awareness of tradition through music and song, and are but a fraction of a large number of available discs. Authentic field recordings are available through the services of the English Folk Dance and Song Society, or with more difficulty through the B.B.C. and various private or semi-private collections. In the U.S.A. the Library of Congress has an immense number of recordings of real folk-music. Commercial recordings, always easily available, should not be separated from their true context of light popular entertainment.

Most of the songs discussed in this book can be heard on long-play records as follows: *Padstow May Song* (Charlie Bate and the Obby Oss Party on 'Folksound of Britain'); *The Bitter Withy* ('Songs of Ceremony' Topic 12T197); *The Leaves of Life* (The Watersons on 'Frost & Fire' Topic 12T136); *Long Langkin, The Two Magicians, Edward, Jackson & Johnson* (all on Bob Stewart, 'The Wraggle Taggle Gypsies O' Crescent ARS 105).

A. L. Lloyd, the folklorist, collector and singer, has made many important recordings, mainly on the Topic label, as have Ewan MacColl & Peggy Seeger, and Anne Briggs; while the Child Ballads I & II are available on Topic 12T160/1.